Power Up wi

Aspirations Rootec

Book One

By Mike Surowiec

Print Edition: ISBN 9798223161318

Power Up With Jesus – Aspirations Rooted in Christ! Book One
By Mike Surowiec

Table of Contents

Other Books by the Author

Unequally Married
Simply The Messenger
Stay Free...Avoid Worldly Traps
Great Business Emulates a Good God
Dancing With God: Life-Giving Theology Explained
Overflowing Prayers Rooted in Jesus Christ v1 & v2
The Adventurous Journey of Transformation in Christ

Dedication

To my fellow apprentices in Christ who are intentionally living out the vision of God's Kingdom.

Scriptural Integration

"We continually ask God to fill you with the knowledge of his will through all the wisdom and understanding that the Spirit gives," (Colossians 1:9)

Introduction

The below Scriptures emphasize our Source of power.

Acts 1:8

But you will receive power when the Holy Spirit has come upon you, and you will be my witnesses in Jerusalem and in all Judea and Samaria, and to the end of the earth."

Romans 15:13

May the God of hope fill you with all joy and peace in believing, so that by the power of the Holy Spirit you may abound in hope.

1 Corinthians 2:5

so that your faith might not rest in the wisdom of men but in the power of God.

1 Corinthians 4:20

For the kingdom of God does not consist in talk but in power.

2 Corinthians 12:9

But he said to me, "My grace is sufficient for you, for my power is made perfect in weakness." Therefore I will boast all the more gladly of my weaknesses, so that the power of Christ may rest upon me.

Ephesians 3:16

that according to the riches of his glory he may grant you to be strengthened with power through his Spirit in your inner being,

2 Timothy 1:7

for God gave us a spirit not of fear but of power and love and self-control.

These aspirations were originally published on my blog. They are now bundled together in one place for a more convenient read. Book one is the start of a series with each book containing 120 short writings. Each aspiration gives you a greater glimpse into the heart of Jesus Christ as the Holy Spirit works to mold us into HIS image. As these lessons have done for me, hopefully, they will also open your eyes and mind to capture God's vision for your life.

As you read, ask God to enlighten you further. To make His Kingdom and ways a daily practice. Also, as HE opens doors for you, learn from the experience. Along the way, may your relationship with the Triune God grow deeper and more trustworthy. You will also find as you grow in the grace and knowledge of Jesus Christ, your soul will more and more reflect HIM unto eternity.

My prayer is for Lord Jesus to intercede for you. To have Father God empower HIS Spirit to fully engage with you so you may experience the power of HIS Ways in your daily walk with HIM.

Remember, we are always rooting for you in Christ!

#1 – Jesus Is Our Reference Point

"Jesus said to him, "I am the way, and the truth, and the life. No one comes to the Father except through me." John 14:6

Most people quote the above scripture to emphasize that Jesus is the only way to salvation. I quote this scripture to let people know through Christ we have a relationship with the Creator God. When we have Jesus as our reference point, life begins to make sense. As we focus on developing a relationship with the Triune God, salvation is the byproduct. When people first focus on salvation, the relationship starts from a contractual arrangement. That is how many people may first accept Christ, yet is it the way He mentored?

In today's world, relationships are being torn apart. We see marriage, friendships, and business partnerships emphasize satisfying the self before others. The reference point becomes the self. This of course leads to a world without Godly influence. Without this influence, the reference point becomes a moving target. This is what has happened in our so called secular world.

Our western world has developed a culture without a reference point. And without a reference point, wise decisions become a hit and miss. The spread of relative morals has likewise produced a foolhardy culture. Again, without a reference point for logical decision making, anything goes. By throwing the Triune God away from the public arena, God is being cancelled. We witness youth and adults question the value of God through the reality of the world around them. Life becomes meaningless. Their questions are unanswered. What good is it to have a relationship with a living God if they don't understand HIS purpose for them?

When people don't have a reference point to refer too, anything goes. History demonstrates over and over again what becomes of a people who forget God. When Jesus said He is the way, life, and truth, He summarized what He brings to the table for humanity. To follow Him, one gains the real treasures of life and builds on the foundation of reality. When He becomes your reference point, your life becomes more purposeful and meaningful. Your ideas, values, and decisions have a measuring stick to weigh outcomes against. You have a mentor, hero, and teacher to show you how to succeed in relationships. To flourish in business. To manage your personal agendas without fear of tomorrow.

When Jesus is your reference point, you read the Bible hungry. You are thirsty to learn everything you can about Him. You align His plans with your goals. You imitate His method of operations. You want to understand His Kingdom, His Church, and His Work. Over time you learn to appreciate everything He has done, is doing, and will be doing. You realize it takes time to build a relationship to know Him, walk with Him, and talk with Him. You realize how blessed you are to have Him as your reference point. Whether heaven arrives tomorrow or not, all you know is that heaven is now when you are engaged with life in Christ.

So ask yourself, which way would you prefer to live? With moving and uncertain world standards or with meaning and purpose in Christ?

#2 – A Mirror Image of Jesus

"And we all, with unveiled face, beholding the glory of the Lord are being transformed into the same image from one degree of glory to another. For this comes from the Lord who is the Spirit." 2 Corinthians 3:18

In Jesus' time, people knew you were a Jew because you kept the law. A visible part of that law was the keeping of the seventh day Sabbath. As a Christ-follower, our sign to the world is not how well we keep the law but how well is Christ formed in us.

What advertises us to the world is a way of life rooted and built on the foundation of Jesus Christ. This life is expressed through the power and love of the Holy Spirit. When people see something different in us, that difference is the heart, mind, and soul of God.

In our relationship with our Heavenly Dad, iron sharpens iron. Our Triune God's influence in our life is changing us to reflect His glory, love, and nature before others. If we are an authentic disciple of Jesus, than isn't Jesus living in us and expressing Himself through us?

When Jesus sees us, isn't our hope and vision that He sees a mirror image of Himself? Though most of us would have to admit that is not always true of us. Aren't there many times a day when the mirror becomes gray, cloudy, and difficult to see? Like many of the saints before us, isn't it a daily discipline to keep the mirror clean? What we find works best is to keep our daily focus on strengthening our relationship with the Triune God.

One of the best analogies is the relationship with our spouse. It started the day I was infatuated with her. It became public knowledge the day we married. From the day we married till today, our love has grown deeper and our relationship stronger. But it didn't happen via fiat. Our relationship grew because we both focused on the disciplines to make it happen. The relationship is important for us. Thus we invest the time in nurturing and enjoying each other's companionship.

Isn't this likewise with God?

He grabbed our attention. He led us to our Lord Jesus. He introduced us to the Holy Spirit. Life has since been one infatuated, passionate journey of discovery and relationship-building.

Just like we will not harm the relationship with our spouse, the same is true with our Eternal Partner. We work hard to strengthen our marriage relationship. We also invest energy to improve our heavenly relationship. It takes time and priority to build a strong marriage. It even takes more time and priority to build a strong relationship with our Invisible God.

Our daily goal is that nothing comes before or between our relationship with each other. When Jesus returns, doesn't our heart, mind, and ears desire to hear His words, "Well done my faithful servant." Until then, we lift our banner as high as we are capable each day. For our banner is Jesus Christ expressing Himself in us and through us each day. Like Paul wrote in the book of Galatians, "I have been crucified with Christ and I no longer live, but Christ lives in me." And with that we say Amen.

#3 - How Can You Best Serve God?

"No one can serve two masters; for either he will hate the one and love the other, or he will be devoted to the one and despise the other. You cannot serve God and mammon [money, possessions, fame, status, or whatever is valued more than the Lord]." Matthew 6:24 (AMP)

Everyone has a master. This may be shocking for those who live in the "free world." For many boasts of their independence and freedom. Yet even in the countries of northern America or western Europe every person has a master. Most often their master is not the governmental system or leader but themselves.

The truth be told each one of us serves our passions and dreams and desires rather than someone else's dictates. Yet Jesus himself states that a person cannot serve two masters. One will be better served than the other. So how do you know you are serving your Lord rather than yourself?

First there are those who serve Jesus for their own self-centered purpose. Generally, they want something and believe if they serve Jesus, he will grant them their wish. Then there are those who have emptied themselves from personal ambition. They truly find joy serving Jesus without a personal agenda. These are the ones who have matured through life. They realize the relationship with God is more valuable than any personal goal.

The first group looks for ways to "buy" God through favors by servicing others. The second group builds a relationship with God to become more aware of His presence. Then they join him with their hands and feet in serving others. Many time they don't even know what they are doing and the impact their service for others mean. They are only grateful and appreciative for the opportunity to work along their Master.

Typically, the second group doesn't look for extra work to perform for God. Instead they know God is already involved in the work they do. Their service is to perform their daily routine for God's glory. A mother or father caring for their children are already glorifying God. They do so through their loving responsibility for their children. The receptionist in the office is already serving God. They are being a joyful representative of His kingdom with everyone they meet. Likewise, the mechanic repairing the client's automobile as if it was his own. They are being truthful and fair in the exceptional work they perform. They are already serving God by witnessing His values before others.

The list is endless. We serve God best by doing what we do every day for His glory. When we exercise the gifts he has bestowed upon us into good, productive work, HE is lifted up. When we perform our service for others in a saintly manner, HE is honored. When we are transparent and caring for the well-being of others, HE is recognized.

You are being a profitable servant in your daily routines. You are introducing God's kingdom to the people around you. You are representing King Jesus as His faithful witness to others. This is one of the best ways to serve our God.

#4 - Where is God's Domain?

And Jesus came and said to them, "All authority in heaven and on earth has been given to me".
Matt. 28:18

One of my disciplines is to read through the Bible each year. Some years though it may take longer than others. It depends on what concepts and verses jump out at me. I'm always amazed to discover something new about God or myself in the process each year.

This past year we read the New Testament from a Greek Lexicon. The Scriptures contain the precise translation of each word in English. In the Book of Matthew, I was surprised to notice the Greek translation "Kingdom of Heaven" was written as "Kingdom of Heavens." The difference of course is the Bible denotes three definitions for heaven. The first is the eternal habitat of God. The second is the sky above the earth. The third is the universal body of stars and planets that surrounds the earth. Why does this matter?

The English translation of "heaven" implies God's government is only effective in his eternal habitat. The Greek manuscript's version "heavens" reinforces God's domain includes all three heavens. A larger domain than just the heaven that is God's abode. Whatever its worth, it reminds us the Bible was not originally written in English. It requires us to do some homework before we accept what is written. This is why it is good to have various translations to provide us with a more complete picture of the author's intent and message.

So next time when we read Matthew's gospel, remember God's kingdom and domain includes the entire heaven, earth, and universe. But then again, you probably already knew that.

#5 - Less Self, More God & Others

"Do nothing from selfishness or empty conceit, but with humility of mind regard one another as more important than yourselves..." Philippians 2:3

Being selfless isn't reducing your worth as a human being. You are created in the image of God and your worth is hidden in Jesus Christ. You are priceless in God's eyes. You are worth more than you even imagine. Your worth isn't measured by what or how you do something; your value is in what Jesus has done, is doing, and yet will do.

Yet, we are instructed to focus our minds to look at others as more important than ourselves. What does that mean?

First being selfless doesn't mean you think you are less important than others. It means you simply spend less time thinking about yourself and your needs. Instead you invest more time thinking how you may better serve others.

The best decisions you make will be a win-win-win scenario. First you will follow God's lead and Will. Then you will want what is best for the other person. Last but not least, you will also want what is best for yourself. There most likely will be compromise. But, the end result will generally be fruitful for everyone involved. Sometimes one side must sacrifice more than the other. But when God is in the picture, sacrificial love is His specialty. And he has a way of rewarding us in serving with Him as He works in the lives of others.

In this world economy, many people have a limited pie view. They don't understand God's economy of multiplication. Jesus took five loaves and two fish to feed 5,000. He directed Peter and his fishing team where to find a large spool of fish that almost flooded the boat. He also fed millions of people during the Exodus where no grocery store was to be found in the area. When serving others, we know we are being held in His Grip. Though we may fall occasionally and be hurt, we also know he is always there to walk us through the situation.

Humility is simply knowing God and the value HE places on all people. This includes you and everyone you meet. Like Jesus, we wash the feet of others because that is the way of God. Our value is in Him. From that perspective, whatever he did and does is what we do. He emptied himself to become human and full of the Holy Spirit. We try to do and be likewise. As we empty ourselves, He makes his home in us and fills us with Himself, the Holy Spirit, and our Father God.

His Kingdom is built on service for others through Him by you. A threefold cord that works wonders in every aspect of life.

#6 - Build Strengths, Compliment Weaknesses

"So do not fear, for I am with you; do not be dismayed, for I am your God. I will strengthen you and help you; I will uphold you with my righteous right hand." Isaiah 41:10

When your performance doesn't measure up to expectations, what do you change? Do you focus on fixing your weaknesses rather than improving your strengths. Good coaches help you to operate around your strengths and compliment your weaknesses.

We see this in sports. Take football as an example. This year, the Cleveland Brown's offense operates on the quarterback's strength. The quarterback, Brian Hoyer's strength is the mid-to-long ball arena. So, the team plays a horizontal game. Here Brian is throwing down field rather than short routes. The short game is his weakness. The long game is his strength. The outcome is Mr. Hoyer leads all quarterbacks in long throw performance ratings. As a result, the Cleveland Browns are in serious contention for a playoff spot. No one gave them a chance in the beginning of the year.

The same is true in business. Almost every single new successful business is built around the entrepreneur's strengths. When the owner starts to deviate away from their core strength, the business starts to falter. The process is usually slow because the owner is trying to save money by doing it herself. The problem is it takes him twice as long to complete the job than someone else whose strength is a perfect match. We see this when a business succeeds on the sales skills of an owner. When he also tries to keep the company books he is travelling outside his area of expertise. Yes he may save a few dollars in the short term. But in the long term he is losing opportunities to sell. And sales is how the company became successful in the first place.

This is also true in leadership. Abraham Lincoln is a good example of someone who understood this principle. When he was elected President, he surrounded himself with the best people knowledgeable in their field of specialty. His cabinet consisted of "political enemies" and "self-seeking" businessmen. He knew his strength was his gift of discernment and communications. Thus, he exercised his primary strength and complimented his weaknesses. He surrounded himself with people to compliment his shortcomings. Most novice leaders surround themselves with like-minded people. President Lincoln was not a novice. He accepted the confrontations and egos. This was the way to provide him with the best support to effectively lead the country.

As disciples, we likewise need to learn to build our lives on our primary strengths. That means the foundation of Jesus Christ is first planted in our life. That we know His Word and enthusiastically follow His Spirit. We accept the natural gifts God has bestowed upon us. Then find ways to express them for God's glory and the sake of others. We also realize our shortcomings. So we surround ourselves with people and boundaries that compliment us. We also always lean on our primary Strength, the Triune God. From HIM, we learn to integrate and grow God's Kingdom through our work, family, and other pursuits.

Life in Christ is most enjoyable when our God-given strengths are employed. There is great joy to work with others advancing His plans. Times like this we experience being fully human. We revert to God's original intended when HE created humankind. When God's Spirit merges with our soul, God's new creation becomes a reality in our world today.

Build Strengths. Compliment Weaknesses. A proven principle that works!

#7 – Difference Between Your Roles and Identity

"If the axe is dull and he does not sharpen its edge, then he must exert more strength. Wisdom has the advantage of giving success." Ecclesiastes 10:10

There is one habit successful people all learn. The trait to convert failure into success. Many people are like an old ax with a dull blade. They continue to exert more physical energy in its use rather than employ sound wisdom. They mimic the person who keeps trying to mop up the water in the bathroom without first turning off the faucet. They work harder rather than smarter. But sound wisdom is available for those who are tired of continually falling short of the mark.

To pursue any type of success without setbacks is like running a marathon without oxygen. Life is not designed that way. The quicker one learns to turn lemons into lemonade, the more enjoyable life will become.

First failure is in the eye of the beholder. Thomas Edison failed over two thousand times to find the perfect filament for the light bulb. That is how an outsider viewed the situation. But, Mr. Edison himself viewed each test as one step to eliminate what doesn't work.

There is one good reason people are able to manage failure. It is the ability to separate their identity from their daily roles. Us humans are made in the image of our Creator. We are a child of the same God who holds the universe together. We are also held in the grip of Jesus Christ. We were made to be morph into his image. You have an eternal identity which no failure nor person can remove.

But when your identity is found in anything else, you have made an idol. In due time, your idol will come crumbling down. It does not matter how good it may look or be.

The goal is to separate your identity from your roles in life. Then you will find it easier to evaluate the situation. You will separate your emotional plugs and come up with more reasonable solutions. But when you use your role as your identity cup, that cup will leave you empty when the role is over. Roles come and go but your identity in Christ remains forever.

You see this all the time. The person whose career is over becomes lost because their identity was buried in their work. The mother whose identity is in her children becomes lost when the children leave home. The teenager whose identity is found with friends becomes lost if not accepted by his peers. The athlete whose identity is found on the football field becomes lost when he is discarded.

When you know who you are in Christ though, then each role you accept becomes a learning process. The means of developing the necessary skills needed to succeed in that role. No matter how well you succeed or fail to succeed, you are only defining your ability to manage that role. Your identity in Christ doesn't change. Yes, you may be a lousy waitress, but you are an awesome child of God. Yes, you may be a lousy ballplayer, but you can improve by sharpening the necessary skills. The same with any role you have chosen to pursue.

Of course, there is an easier route. Build your role upon the God-given gifts and natural abilities given. Align them with the people you want to serve. Where these qualities intersect with your interest is your sweet spot. Then exercise motivation and hard work to develop the necessary skills. You may not become the #1 rated person in your industry, but you will be highly respected for what and how you do it.

So, the next time you find yourself short of your mark, thank God. Thank HIM for the opportunity you have been given. Then find yourself a mentor. Identify your strengths and weaknesses. Build on your strengths. Complement your weaknesses. Establish your goals. Start your journey. Remember, failure only sets the bar for you to discover what you need to change. Learn, integrate, and grow to become more effective in the role you are working through.

Don't confuse your identity with your role. Master your role. Keep centered in your identity. Then failure is only a holding pattern in a learning process of improving your role.

#8 - God Is Working Everything for Your Good

"And we know that for those who love God all things work together for good, for those who are called according to his purpose." Romans 8:28

How do you define good? When do you determine something is either good or bad?

If life throws a curve ball at you when you were expecting a fast ball, was that a good pitch or not? Don't our shortsighted expectations sometimes blind us to reality?

Generally, we believe something is good almost immediately after its impact. For example, when we slam on our brakes at the last second to avoid a serious head-on-accident by inches. Or when we are looking for a job. Then ones comes from nowhere. An offer with a higher salary and responsibilities than you ever imagined. Or when you feel a lump on your breast and receive that phone call from your doctor acknowledging it is benign.

All these events end with immediate good news.

Yes, the news is good. And for the minute we celebrate. Yet what about those times when the events stink.

When your fiancée breaks up with you one week before the wedding.

When your tire goes flat ten minutes away from an important interview for the job of your dreams.

When the candidate you lobbied for and voted for fails to win the election.

At times like this you feel your world has come to an end. You are disappointed and maybe even angry at God for not protecting you from such "harm." But are these events necessary "bad." Or are they temporary, eye-opening moments to refocus our attention on the God of the universe. HE who is constantly working for every person's best; even when they don't want it.

Your trust in God will be challenged by the unpleasant events in your life. Yet you will come to know him more intimately and personally as you place your undivided trust in Him. Whether you are thrown into a fiery pit. Whether you stand before a large army attacking your front and a large lake blocks your retreat. Or your nine-foot goliath stands in front of you with heavy military armor and you only have a sling shot. Your immediate response may be "this isn't good." Yet, you will recall all the times your God intervene and the outcome was better than you could ever expect. Or the times you may have suffered for years. But in hindsight you realize those "bad" years were the best time of spiritual growth. You invested greater time in your interpersonal relationship with your Heavenly Father.

One day we come to realize no matter what happens in life, God is always at work for your good and mine. Sometimes we have to wait longer than desired. Yet other times He delivers before we even know what happened.

God is good. All the time. Sometimes it takes time to realize the goodness of the situation.

#9 - Love Has No Agenda

"It(love) does not insist on its own way" I Corinthians 13:5

Love is one of those words that has become cheaper through cultural opinion. Ask for a definition, and you will probably receive a multitude of answers. In today's culture, it means different things for different folks.

For teenagers, it is the emotional tie that binds two people together until the feeling goes away. For newlyweds, it is the blindness that denies the imperfection of the other. For testosterone husbands, it is the words for a sexual encounter. For manipulative wives, it is the means to get what they may want.

Yet Paul writes that love is not something we get, but give.

Jesus gives us the perfect example of what love means in a very practical everyday way. To sacrifice the self for the sake of the other is love demonstrated. It is giving the self for the sake of others. It is not giving so others may agree with you. It is not giving so others do something for you. It is not giving so you may benefit from it at all. In fact, it may hurt to give. It may cost you your job. It may cost you a relationship. It may cost you your life.

Your response measures the love you have to give. It is what Jesus did for us. He set the example. He chose to empty his eternal habitat so he could walk among us. He gave himself as a sacrifice, so we can enter his eternal home.

We can either love or deny what it truly means from his context. So the next time you let someone know you love them, what are you going to sacrifice? Are you willing to give your time, money, and life for them without any expectations in return? Whatever your response, you now know what God knows about us. And even knowing this, He still unconditionally loves you and me.

He loves us whether we choose to follow him. Yes he wants us to respond to him in a favorable way. Yet if we do not, he still loves us. We may suffer the consequences of our rebellious attitude. Yet our response doesn't stop Him from loving us. We may suffer from our stupidity. But He remains steadfast in His love for us. Isn't that the Christ-like love we need to display?

#10 – Favor of the Lord

"In the sixth month the angel Gabriel was sent from God to a city of Galilee named Nazareth, to a virgin betrothed to a man whose name was Joseph, of the house of David. And the virgin's name was Mary. And he came to her and said, "Greetings, O favored one, the Lord is with you!" But she was greatly troubled at the saying, and tried to discern what sort of greeting this might be. And the angel said to her, "Do not be afraid, Mary, for you have found favor with God. And behold, you will conceive in your womb and bear a son, and you shall call his name Jesus." Luke 1:26-31

Sometimes we hold unto blissful expectations which soon become painful disappointments. Take the concept of wanting to experience the favor of the Lord. Most humans would desire the favor of the Lord. We picture ourselves sitting on a royal chair with subjects. Enjoying a life of ease and comfort. All our desires satisfied. Yet reality speaks differently as Jesus' mother Mary experienced through her life.

Yes, she was favored by the Lord to be the birth mother of the Son of God. But life wasn't a bowl of peaches because of it. Think of all she had to endure through the process?

She was a pregnant unmarried woman living in a small village. Generally in small towns everybody knows everyone else's business. Per the old Jewish oracles, a woman without a husband and pregnant was to be stoned to death. How favored of a life is it to live under a death threat? Where you are living out each day hiding your condition from those around you? Your parents, siblings, and neighbors ready to condemn you to death. What about spending the last month of your pregnancy riding a donkey and walking every day? She and Joseph travelled for 80 miles from Nazareth to Bethlehem to take part in a census. Then to give birth in a non-sanitized environment without support of family. Is this the favored life?

To be favored by God is a blessing. You know He has your back. But the process of every day challenges and threats still remain. To be favored by God is an adventurous life and not necessarily a safe one. Yet to know you are being held in His Grip through all the ups and downs life throws your way is a blessing. For HE is a comfort to the soul.

Even with suffering or pain that comes our way, I rather be favored by God than not. How about you?

#11 - What is God's Greatest Expression of His Love?

"Who is the man who desires life and loves length of days that he may see good?" Psalm 34:12

Life. God created you for eternal habitation with Him. Without life you wouldn't know God, family, nor anything. You wouldn't exist. In my opinion, Life is God's greatest expression of His Love. He created the universe to be inhabited. He created earth to be inhabited with humans. His desire is for humanity to share in His life. Everything created by Him is love being fulfilled. Without life, there is no experience of love, God, nor anything.

Even when humanity rebelled against Him, He intervened. He elected Himself as an atoning sacrifice. Jesus Christ is God's continual expression of his love for us. God came in flesh to experience life in human skin. He now has a better understanding of you and me because he lived it out. Christ's entire life was lived out so you and I could see how life is meant to be lived. His life, death, and resurrection culminated into our relationship being restored with God.

Life comes only from life. Science has not yet discovered the missing link where matter becomes life. Even they acknowledge that life is born only from a living entity. As the Book of Genesis stated, God breathed into man and he became a living soul. As physical life only comes from physical life, eternal life only comes from eternal life. As Jesus stated to Nicodemus, one must be born again by the Spirit. Life comes from life.

God's greatest gift to humanity is life. He created physical life with people with free-will because He wanted to share his life and love with each of us. But relationship is a two-way street. It takes two to tango. God freely gives us life and waits to see if we want to share life with Him. For those who do, eternal life awaits them. For those who do not want to be in relationship with Him, he will oblige. Hopefully, you have come to a point in your world where God's love wins you over. For after you have a small taste of His love and life, you can't live without. He is Love and Life in one.

#12 – You Are Included

"For by grace you have been saved through faith. And this is not your own doing; it is the gift of God..." Ephesians 2:8

One difference between mainline Christian denominations is understanding when you are saved

Arminianism theology believes you are saved when you make the election to choose God. Calvinism theology believes God has already predetermined your life's final destination. Then Trinitarian theology believes God has already chosen you. But you need to exercise faith to experience the fruit of salvation.

I find adoption theology gives a good example of explaining the differences.

Under adoption theology, God through Christ has adopted humanity. This through HIS life, death, and resurrection. Just like a parent adopts a child into the family fold, God has adopted humanity into the family circle.

The child either accepts their position as a new family member, or not. Upon acceptance they become engaged with the family culture. The child is already included within the family whether they accept their role or not. Their actions are either to accept the family or rebel. When they accept, they enjoy the fruit of family living. If they rebel, they still are a family member. But lost from sharing life with the family and the family treasures.

Arminianism theology teaches that the child selects the parent for adoption. You are not included in the family until you decide to make it so. The parent only offers adoption, and the child is the one who legally binds the offer. The weight is on the child choosing to be adopted or not.

Calvinism theology teaches that God has adopted some and has not adopted others. Some will experience eternity with God and others are predestinated for eternal lost. As a child, you have to figure out whether you are included or excluded from God's family.

My bias is toward Trinitarian theology. Salvation is what Jesus accomplished and not what we make happen. Salvation is more about a familial relationship with the living God. Salvation is not a business transaction.

There are those who treat salvation as something you earn by achieving a goal. Others think salvation is keeping score of good behavior. Than some count their noble actions toward others.

Salvation is about being included within the Eternal God's circle of Father-Son-Spirit. When you realize this, salvation changes your perspective of God, family, and life.

Paul writes that God chose humanity before the foundation of the world. The purpose is to become his children (Eph. 1-4-5). When Christ rose from the dead, he not only defeated death for himself, but included all humanity with him. Our home is with him. You cannot be lost unless you already have a home. Those who don't truly know Jesus Christ yet have a home waiting for them. They have already been adopted into the family but don't realize the riches that await them. When they accept Jesus and His lordship, life changes. They become engaged in the Family business and enjoy the fruit of God's redemptive plan.

But some will continue to rebel against participating in God's family endeavors. Their choice is not to be engaged with Christ. Then there will be unpleasant consequences; including the loss of everlasting life.

Our chose is not whether we want to be adopted. Our chose is whether we want to accept our position within the family. Whether we want to participate in God's family business. You are already included. The question then becomes, what are you going to do about it?

#13 - God's Purpose For You

"My children, with whom I am again in labor until Christ is formed in you" Galatians 4:19

Whenever another message is preached that God has a plan for you, I cringe. Most often, not always, but most often the message comes across that you are unique (true). You have one specific life role God designed you for (maybe). If you dream it, it must be from God (maybe). And your earthly destiny is already planned out (ouch).

Now we could discuss free-will and predestination, but will not. That is a never-ending discussion subject to your preliminary worldview. But we will agree that God does have a plan for your life. It involves every aspect of your goals, dreams, passion, and purpose. That goal is to form Christ in you!

These Scriptures record the apostle's Paul emphasis on Christ being formed in you. Galatians 2:20, Ephesians 3:14:19, Ephesians 4:11-19, Philippians 3:21, and Colossians 1:28.

So, have you already submitted yourself under Christ's authority? If so, then HE will continue to transform your character through the Holy Spirit. This allows you to pursue the goals, dreams, and passions you desire as long as healthy morals are in play.

When you live in the center of God's Will, rarely will your choice be predetermined rebellion against Him. Instead your options are like Adam and Eve's. How many trees were available for them to focus their attention on? Wasn't the tree of life also in the garden with the tree of knowledge of good and evil? So, why did they select the one God told them not too? Life choices are many. But as long as you hold unto the One Who Is the Source of Life, you will be OK. God's plan is to bring you unto maturity in Christ.

The God we serve is so much larger than you and I can ever phantom. He allows us to exercise free-will. As we do, He continues the process of changing us. From a self-centered, self-ruled person to a Christ-centered, spirit-led adopted child of His.

If fact, the more Christ is formed in you, the more options come your way. You come to realize there isn't one physical goal, one dream, or one passion with your name on it. Instead you have the entire galaxy at your disposal. Only our limited thinking narrows the possibilities in front of us. Our doubtful trust in God, fear of failure, and shortsightedness are our roadblocks.

God's desire is to develop your leadership skills. To live out HIS Kingdom-centered values. To partner with Jesus Christ via the Holy Spirit. To mature you in Him. To exercise personal judgement. To gather counsel from your elders that know you. To discover and choose the path your passion, talents, and love for others lead you. You can be assured God is always with you. HE will continue to form you in the image of His Son along the way.

#14 - Jesus' Priority for Daily Living

'Our Father who is in heaven,
Hallowed be Your name.
'Your kingdom come.
Your will be done,
On earth as it is in heaven.
'Give us this day our daily bread.
'And forgive us our debts, as we also have forgiven our debtors.
'And do not lead us into temptation, but deliver us from evil. For Yours is the kingdom and the power and the glory forever. Amen.' Matt 6:9-13

We can view Jesus' priority of values by viewing the prayer he taught his students. Today we classify this prayer as The Lord's Prayer. When you study this prayer, you notice the hierarchy of values Jesus places on each request. Each request identifies an important value for living. Also they move from the highest to the lowest of importance.

First, HE identifies we are all together on this life voyage by recognizing God as Father of us all. Translation: life is a team sport and God is the owner and coach.

Secondly, HE gives great respect and tribute to God for who He IS and what His name signifies. Translation: God is creator and humanity is his creation – acknowledge it and live it out.

The third point Jesus emphasizes is God's Kingdom coming to earth. Translation: His message to earth's inhabitants is the reign of God's Kingdom being restored on earth. So get on board. His government rules through the souls of his subjects. They execute his decrees from a servant's heart.

The fourth point highlights the importance of maintaining the attitude of a servant. To follow the desires and wishes of his master. Translation: the emphasis is for you to do whatever you do God's way and place your desires and wishes behind His. You are a servant of the Lord for the sake of others.

The next point highlights how Jesus places importance of colonizing earth. We are not to wait until we are all in heaven, but focus on bringing the richness of heaven to earth today. Translation: your everyday mission is to colonize earth.

After focusing on God's priorities, Jesus then place the need of physical necessities. Translation: we all need food, clothing, and shelter. Since God created all the resources at our disposal, HE can also lead us to them.

Then his emphasis is on relationships. Translation: we mend relationships by forgiving others. Through forgiveness, we learn humility and love for God, others and ourselves.

Next, he acknowledges the struggle of temptations. These may turn into a sorry state of affairs IF not defeated. Translation: be not blind to the strength of sin's influence. Proactively keep asking for help to keep these battles far from us and minimal in quantity.

He also acknowledges the evil around us. Translation: this alone should prompt us to keep in close contact with Him who can help us in times of trouble.

And lastly, HE closes where he began. By acknowledging God is here forever and His kingdom is forever, and His rule is forever, and His fame is forever. Translation: HE is the One who needs to remain the center of everything we think, do, and want to be. Life is His story being played out through humanity.

Final thought: Jesus taught this prayer to highlight the important priorities of God. Is it possible the needs of mankind work hand-in-hand with His ultimate plan for humanity?

#15 – What New Creation?

"Therefore, if anyone is in Christ, he is a new creation. The old has passed away; behold, the new has come." 2 Corinthians 5:17

Do we understand what the new creation is all about? When we look at ourselves in the mirror of Jesus, do we recognize a new creation? How does the new creation come about?

Most of us don't get into the details of life in Christ. We just accept what we read or hear. Yet some of us want to know more. We desire to know the heart of God. We thirst to understand His purpose. We hunger for the wisdom to express God's character wherever we go.

When Jesus died, resurrected, and ascended into heaven, HE became the first born of a new creation. The first man to morph into a heavenly being. His physical flesh changed into a spiritual entity. A person with the ability to eat physical food and also walk through physical doors. He was the first of many who are yet waiting for their resurrection.

Today we only capture a glimpse of that reality through marriage. The marriage institute of man and woman pictures the relationship of a new creation. As Jesus mentioned in Scripture (Mt. 19:5), a man leaves his parents and clings to his wife - where the two become one flesh. A healthy marriage is when both the man and woman live life sacrificing the self. They give 100% for the other with the purpose of creating a new entity. Two people operating in harmony and united as one new entity.

As we are included in Christ because of His new work for us, we join him in his new venture. For now, he has done and is doing his part. We are now learning to give 100% to him in response to his love for us. As we deny ourselves and allow him to bathe us with his Spirit, we part take in His new creation. The two of us are becoming one.

So now we can enjoy his life and participate with him as HE shares his new life with us. Yes you are a new creation. You are no longer dead, but alive in Him. A new creation tasting His fruit now while waiting to be fully revealed at your resurrection.

#16 - Fulfill Your Potential

"If I speak with the tongues of men and of angels, but do not have love, I have become a noisy gong or a clanging cymbal. If I have the gift of prophecy, and know all mysteries and all knowledge; and if I have all faith, so as to remove mountains, but do not have love, I am nothing. And if I give all my possessions to feed the poor, and if I surrender my body to be burned, but do not have love, it profits me nothing.
Love is patient, love is kind and is not jealous; love does not brag and is not arrogant, does not act unbecomingly; it does not seek its own, is not provoked, does not take into account a wrong suffered, does not rejoice in unrighteousness, but rejoices with the truth; bears all things, believes all things, hopes all things, endures all things.
Love never fails; but if there are gifts of prophecy, they will be done away; if there are tongues, they will cease; if there is knowledge, it will be done away. For we know in part and we prophesy in part; but when the perfect comes, the partial will be done away. When I was a child, I used to speak like a child, think like a child, reason like a child; when I became a man, I did away with childish things. For now we see in a mirror dimly, but then face to face; now I know in part, but then I will know fully just as I also have been fully known." 1Corinthians 13:1-12 (NASB)

The poets, romantics, and song writers have it right. Real love is the greatest high this life offers. We are not speaking of puppy love, or a self-centered feeling which makes you feel good. But a sacrificial, outgoing concern for the welfare and benefit of the other. The love Jesus demonstrated throughout his life.

For example, Lord Jesus washed the feet of his students. A role the lowest of servants of a house usually performed. He forgave his persecutors while dying on the cross. He turned water into wine in respect for his mother. He obliged her so the bride and groom would not be embarrassed at their wedding festivities.

He spent days and nights sacrificing his privacy teaching his students the ways of God. In fact, his entire mission was to introduce everyone to the God he knew. His fulfillment of all prophecy on the messiah was so his God would be honored. His life aim was for humanity to have their relationship with their Creator restored.

He loved truth and spoke the truth in love. His ability to reveal God's goodness with words and actions was a never ending story-line. The apostle John writes in his gospel that you couldn't write enough books to outline them all.

He didn't pursue wealth, marriage, fame, nor power during time on earth. Instead, he was true to himself, his mission, and his God. He knew where he came from, where he was going, and the road of suffering he would have to endure. Yet he didn't have a daily pity party. Instead HE trusted Him who he loved and knew He was loved by Him. Him being his Father and our Father, God Almighty.

He didn't point people to Scripture but pointed Scripture to His Father. His prayer the evening of his betrayal acknowledges his joy of revealing HIS God to others. HIS desire was for all others may also come to know Him. His entire life and mission included making the love of God known.

Do you think there might be more to the X-mas story than just a baby being born so he may die for mankind? Is it possible Jesus came to also reveal what a real fulfilled life looks like?

Could this be a possibility? That experiencing and knowing real love is the fulfillment of our potential?

#17 – Rest in Christ

"Come to me, all who labor and are heavy laden, and I will give you rest. Take my yoke upon you, and learn from me, for I am gentle and lowly in heart, and you will find rest for your souls. For my yoke is easy, and my burden is light." Matt. 11:28-30

Martin Luther was the initiator of the Protestant reformation movement. He was a monk in the Catholic Church struggling to find God. Like many of his contemporaries, he would pray, fast, and subdue his body. All this to seek answers and direction from God. Yet as each practice forced him toward God only led him to become more despondent. Then God in His almighty mercy and grace revealed to him the truth. When that moment occurred, Martin Luther discovered real peace for his soul. Just like the Scriptures promises for those who find rest in Christ.

God blessed him by opening his eyes to understand grace through faith in Christ.

In Jesus time, the religious leaders decoded Scripture into 613 rules for living. These practices became the order of importance. Over time, these rules would measure their righteousness before God and man. Many of these rules became a duty and burden for the people. The people felt pressured to perform or be ostracized from their community. God's freedom escaped them.

Jesus frowned upon this and gave the people an alternative way to live life. Thereby Jesus makes the above statement. He lifts the burden from people's shoulders. His teachings gives them the Rest they want. The same Rest God originally intended mankind to have before Adam's rebellion.

Instead of focusing on DOING a long list of things, Jesus stressed having a relationship with Him. The Rest comes from following Christ; in BEING in a relationship with Him. When you realize who Jesus is and what Jesus has done for you, you begin to experience His Rest.

He is our Substitute. He is our Savior. He is our King. When you accept and begin to believe Him, then and only then, will we begin to experience the joy of His Spirit. You will appreciate Him living in you and the freedom He shares with all His subjects.

Jesus does not put burdens on people; people put burdens on each other. Jesus provides uplifting, refreshing joy. His ways allow people to fulfill their design in Him. He wants people to experience the same joy He does. When we connect with Him, follow Him, serve Him, and rejoice with Him, then we experience Him. The abiding relationship of being one with Him, the Father, and the Holy Spirit leads to a more fruitful life. For where God is, there is abundant Rest. Isn't that what we mean to be radical in Christ?

#18 – Learn to Love

"A new commandment I give to you, that you love one another, even as I have loved you, that you also love one another." John 13:34

Some things are easier to learn than others. Learning to eat comes quite easy. Walking may take a few tries. But most toddlers ignore the bumps and bruises and wander their way about. Learning to swim or bike may take a little longer but most people who attempt it manage to get by. But somethings are just harder than others.

Take Love.

Most of us in our early days think love is how one feels about someone. It is an emotional high that we can't get enough. When the feeling goes away, we look for someone else to fill the hole.

Yet as we mature, most of us learn that love is an action with a heartfelt attitude toward another. It's more about the other person than the self. In fact, the self only gets in the way to express love the way God does.

Take Jesus Christ.

The night before his crucifixion most of us would be having a self-pity party. But HE chose to wash the feet of his disciples before observing the Passover meal with them. Usually this work was done by the house servants. But Jesus demonstrated from his heart what humility looks like. HE showed how serving one another is love in action.

For most of us, we choose who we love and who we refrain from loving. Yet, to become perfect like our heavenly Father, we all need to learn how to love everyone. He does.

So yes, life's lessons include learning to love the obnoxious associate from work. The loud, partying neighbor. Also the aggressive drivers on the freeway. And one can't forget the narcissistic boss. Learning to love those who are like us is easy. But learning to love those whose behaviors and values we disdain, can be challenging.

Jesus loved everyone. Even the religious self-righteous. How well are we learning?

Just another reason to lean more heavily on Christ.

#19 - The Prosperous Soul

"Beloved, I pray that in all respects you may prosper and be in good health, just as your soul prospers." 3 John 1:2

The apostle John wrote a letter to his local church. He gave them the reassurance God wants each one of his children to prosper. Not only spiritually, but also physically. The challenge though is how more people emphasize the physical objectives of life. They ignore the spiritual. They want the benefits of a healthy spiritual walk, but don't want to invest the time and effort.

The prosperous life is so much more than physical comforts. You could gain the whole world, but be poor in spirit. You could have beauty, power, and fame, but be empty, frustrated, and lonely.

A disciple's walk with his Teacher is life enriched. You gain confidence, boldness, and humility. Her life radiates from an inner peace of contentment. The material items that surround her are only means to experience the richness of God's creation.

To be healthy is a blessing. But to be healthy for self-aggrandizement is pompous and vain. Health is a physical and mental condition. Both though are empowered by the soul. A soul that is rich in love, joy, patience, goodness, kindness, and self-control. The essence of God's character is displayed through a soul that is in constant contact with Him.

A soul rich in spiritual blessings is the master of the physical comforts around them. The computer, television, and smart phone are tools being managed by the soul keeper. A rich soul is not addicted to the toys around him. Instead the rich soul manages the comforts of life for a greater purpose.

A rich soul likewise treasures the body as a temple for His divine presence. Thus her attitude is to maintain and operate the body's functions for the long haul. She will not glorify it but discipline it. She will praise its Creator and sustain it for His glory.

Whatever the enriched soul pursues, he does so with the intent to make it better than before. Whether mind, body, or soul, the desire is to magnify the Creator. The enriched soul is not self-made. Instead, the prosperous soul knows Her Creator. She thanks Him in gratitude, and humbly walks with those around Him for their benefit and purpose.

So, whatever your hand finds to do, do it with all you might. Prosper in your health, in your bank account, and in your relationships. But always remember your priorities and your most important function today. God knows. So do you.

#20 – Gratitude 101

"Every good and perfect gift is from above, coming down from the Father of the heavenly lights, who does not change like shifting shadows." James 1:17

Gratitude is an attitude of repentance. Repentance is a mind-set realizing one needs to lock unto the God of the universe. To change one's thinking from a self-centered perspective into a Christ-center worldview.

Repentance is acknowledgement the self is not the center of the universe. That there is Someone greater than self. Someone who made everything possible. The byproduct is a position of humility reflected through one's attitude.

When one begins this journey, one finds many reasons to be thankful.

Thankful for knowing one's blessing is not necessarily due to one's superior talent. Nor one's above average intelligence. Nor one's persuasive demeanor. But thankful for being at the right place and the proper time with the ideal people to bring it all about.

Thankful for realizing how blessed one is for being born this time in history.

Thankful for appreciating all the people in your life. Especially those who contributed toward your success to date.

Thankful for knowing that we are not dead trees blowing in the wind. That God shares His life with us and Spirit which enriches us every day.

Thankful for realizing everything was created by Christ for Christ and through Christ. And HE shares Himself with us.

Thankful for appreciating our value in Christ.

Thankful for knowing the truth which leads to freedom and contentment.

Thankful for realizing our potential as a person. That everything good comes from God. We get to reveal HIM through our work and relationships.

Thankful for appreciating who we are in relationship with others. That we are all likewise included in Christ.

There is much to be thankful for as we travel through the day. To know and see HIS goodness throughout the day. To share HIS gifts with others. To learn more about HIM.

HE turns everyday mundane routine activities into joy. How? Because He is involved with you through it all.

Gratitude 101 is the basic foundation of coming to appreciate God's involvement in your life. How thankful are you?

#21 - Walk It Out With Jesus Christ

"And we know that for those who love God all things work together for good, for those who are called according to his purpose." Romans 8:28

One day you will come to the place in your life where you realize that our heavenly Father wants what is best for you. That HE wants to bless you more than you will ever realize. That no matter what happens, you will always place your trust in Him. You will walk through the situation with a swagger that even your enemies admire.

Your walk is built upon the fact that you seek His purpose in your life. You constantly watch how the Holy Spirit is working in the lives of those around you. Your prayer is for those around you to experience the love of God in their life. Over time you learn through the ups and downs of everyday life that He is with you. You acknowledge His favor. You celebrate His grace. You seek out His purpose each day.

When you serve others you learn to serve with Jesus rather than for Jesus. You first ask Him how you can best serve your brothers and sisters. You read His Word to discover more of His ways. You are His disciple and thus want to act, think, and live out your life like Him. And like Him, you seek His Father's Will.

In placing your daily trust in Him, you have assurance. No matter how ugly the current situation is, it is temporary. God will produce good from it. Not only for your sake, but for those around you, and for His purpose. In the end, God is glorified and His Goodness is shared with others.

It all begins when we learn to walk out our plans, hopes, and dreams with Jesus. Not solely for your sake or others, nor for Him, but with Him.

#22 – The Bible's Wisdom

"How blessed is the man who finds wisdom and the man who gains understanding." Proverbs 3:13

If you are an atheist, what benefit would you receive from reading the Bible? There are some who believe the Book is outdated and has no relevance in the 21st century. Others believe science has replaced the folklore of yesterday. Yet when one studies this number one seller, you realize nothing has really changed from 4,000 years ago. Except for the advancement of technology and fashion. Otherwise, human nature has been the same since the beginning of history.

You discover this Book outlines gems of wisdom for all areas of life. Do you want to learn ways to improve your marriage? Add flavor to your relationships at work and home? Or how government works best? You can find the answers throughout this Book.

You will find wisdom to create wealth, build a business, and invest for the future.

You will find diet tips, money tips, and life tips.

You will find answers for life's tough questions.

You will discover a God who cares, plans, and has a purpose for His creation.

You will discover the mind of God.

You don't have to be a believer to enjoy the lessons and principles taught throughout its pages.

Sometimes the more one becomes "educated", the more common sense seems to disappear. This Book restores common sense. It heightens the importance of knowledge that leads to understanding and wisdom.

There are a whole number of other knowledge building categories for you to sharpen. History. War. Family squabbles. Relationship challenges. Work success. Financial stewardship. Non-penalized fun. Humor. Your Life skill set is sewn between the pages.

So, if you want more wisdom in your life, than read the Book. And if you are open to the experience, you may even discover the real Source of Wisdom.

#23 – Values. Needs. Dreams.

"Can two walk together, unless they are agreed?" Amos 3:3 (NKJV)

What brings people together? What makes two people from an entire universe become friends? Why are some people repulsive to each other?

These are very complex questions which social scientists have done elaborate studies on. Yet when you make it simple and to the point, don't two people come together when they have something in common? Most of the time it may be a task, or an interest, or simply a need to be fulfilled.

I like to think when two people have similar values, needs, or dreams, you have a connection. The potential of developing a real friendship. Sometimes the friendship may lead to a deep bond like marriage. Other times, towards a relationship closer than a brother or sister.

Jesus surrounded himself with twelve disciples. Some were self-employed as fishermen, one a tax collector, and another a terrorist. Most likely these people would have little in common. They probably wouldn't spend much time together for no other reason except for Jesus Christ. What brought them all together? They saw the values, needs, and dreams Jesus expressed as something they desired. They believed Jesus would help them succeed at it.

So, if you are looking for friendship, a mate, or a business relationship, here is your aim. Focus on the other person's values, needs, and dreams. See how they relate with yours. If there is a common thread, you may have hit the jackpot. If not, pray about it. Let the Holy Spirit reveal what you may suspect or show you something deeper that is invisible to the naked eye. Either way, lean on the Triune God and He will show you the way.

At the end of the day, isn't Jesus someone who we all see as a person whose values we admire. Whose ways meet our needs, and who may help us fulfill our dreams?

#24 – Celebrate Life

"For whoever is joined with all the living, there is hope; surely a live dog is better than a dead lion."
Ecclesiastes 9:4

As long as you are alive, you have hope for the future. No matter your circumstances, God's grace abounds everywhere. Nothing is hidden from Him. Nothing escapes Him. Nothing limits Him. He created you to live life to the fullest; to experience His love, and fulfill your potential.

Our challenge most often is to get out of the way. The self thinks our plans and solutions are always the best ones. We fail to admit there may be a better way. Our pride and insecurity often prevents us from yielding ourselves to His instructions. We fail to believe no one knows us better than ourselves. We close our eyes so often to how blind and ignorant the self can become. We all need a mentor. Someone who has gone before us and can show us how to succeed.

Life is for the living, not for the dead. As long as we are alive, we can celebrate the life given to us by our Creator. We may not enjoy our current situation. The circumstances may be in stink mode, but we have hope in a Savior – His name is Jesus.

He lived life to the fullest. He introduced us to His Father. He taught us the reality of life in His Kingdom. He intervenes for us. He shares His life with us. He gives us purpose and meaning to celebrate life the way our Creator designed the world to be.

Yes, there will be disappointments. Yes, expectations fail. Yes, circumstances change. But through everything, the Triune God cares for you and wants you to share in HIS life. As we lean on Him, His character, divine nature, and attributes rubs unto you. You become more of a "little Christ." The joy and peace He instills in you begins to overflow unto others. Your love for others is more fully expressed in your desire to help them succeed. Life becomes more than about survival. Life becomes a celebration of what God has done, is doing, and will yet do.

Always remember, as long as you are alive, you have hope for the future. Why? Because God's Love is greater than anything this world throws your way! This is our reason for celebrating life each and every day.

#25 - By Love, For Love, To Love

"And so we know and rely on the love God has for us. God is love. Whoever lives in love lives in God, and God in them." 1 John 4:16 (NIV)

Love created you, sustains you, and motivates you. You were created by Love, for Love, to Love!

God is Love. His divine character exhibits love. His entire nature freely expresses love independent of what you and I do. He loves because He is love.

When you begin to realize the love He has for you, your assurance and trust in Him grows. When your relationship grows with Him, your love matures to a whole new level.

The day will come when you realize God's purpose for you is to know Him and experience life with Him, and through Him. The outcome includes immeasurably more love than a person can naturally handle.

Love moves the world. You and I do more in the name of love than we admit. We may not understand what real love is until we have an encounter with Him. HE has revealed love to us through Jesus. Jesus is the expressive embodiment of God in human form.

Scripture introduces to us the many ways Jesus expressed His Father's love. He had an intimate relationship with the Godhead as a Son. His pre-public ministry including serving in Joseph's family carpentry business. Upon his arrival to be baptized by John, he lived His vicarious life from beginning to end for you, me, and His Father. He healed, taught, and gave himself in service so others may come to know who His Father is truly like.

Without love there is no hope, no future, nor joy. With love, everything is more colorful, adventurous, and meaningful. Your passion for whatever is a byproduct of channeled love. Your hobbies, your work, and the mate you choose all are avenues to express your love.

Yet love is not only about you. Love includes everyone. God. Family. Friends. Associates. Neighbors. Country. Men. Women. Every person who arrives on planet earth. Yes, even your enemies.

Real love is sacrificial and up-building. The Triune God birth humanity from the central core of love. The entire universe is built upon the natural laws govern by love. Love rules the galaxies. This is why love is the most important attribute of life.

So always remember: You were created by Love, for Love, to Love!

#26 – Evil

"The fear of the Lord is hatred of evil. Pride and arrogance and the way of evil and perverted speech I hate." Proverbs 8:13

Because of the recent terrorist attacks, I did a short, old-fashion review from the Bible on the word evil. Rather than write something in my own words, below is a short review of these Scriptures.

"Evil men do not understand justice, but those who seek the Lord understand it completely." Proverbs 28:5

"Deceit is in the heart of those who devise evil, but those who plan peace have joy." Proverbs 12:20

"Woe to those who call evil good and good evil, who put darkness for light and light for darkness, who put bitter for sweet and sweet for bitter!" Isaiah 5:20

"Their feet run to evil, and they are swift to shed innocent blood; their thoughts are thoughts of iniquity; desolation and destruction are in their highways." Isaiah 59:7

"Hate evil, and love good, and establish justice in the gate; it may be that the Lord, the God of hosts, will be gracious to the remnant of Joseph. Amos 5:15

"When God saw what they did, how they turned from their evil way, God relented of the disaster that he had said he would do to them, and he did not do it." Jonah 3:10

"...do not devise evil in your hearts against one another, and love no false oath, for all these things I hate, declares the Lord." Zechariah 8:17

"You brood of vipers! How can you speak good, when you are evil? For out of the abundance of the heart the mouth speaks. The good person out of his good treasure brings forth good, and the evil person out of his evil treasure brings forth evil." Matthew 12:34-35

"For out of the heart come evil thoughts, murder, adultery, sexual immorality, theft, false witness, slander." Matthew 15:19

"Repay no one evil for evil, but give thought to do what is honorable in the sight of all." Romans 12:21

"Let love be genuine. Abhor what is evil; hold fast to what is good." Romans 12:9

"For we must all appear before the judgment seat of Christ, so that each one may receive what is due for what he has done in the body, whether good or evil. 2 Corinthians 5:10

"Abstain from every form of evil." 1 Thessalonians 5:22

"But the Lord is faithful. He will establish you and guard you against the evil one." 2 Thessalonians 3:3

"The Lord will rescue me (Paul) from every evil deed and bring me safely into his heavenly kingdom. To him be the glory forever and ever." Amen. 2 Timothy 4:18

"Beloved, do not imitate evil but imitate good. Whoever does good is from God; whoever does evil has not seen God." 3 John 1:11

#27 – Sacredness

"If the part of the dough offered as first fruits is holy, then the whole batch is holy; if the root is holy, so are the branches." Romans 11:16

What makes something secular or sacred? Holy or unholy?

The culture around us likes to put everything into little boxes. There are religious boxes. Government boxes. Business boxes. Family boxes. Internet boxes. You name it and there is a box for it. Dependent on how religious or nonreligious we are, we also have boxes for what is secular and what is sacred.

Yet who or what determines if something is sacred or secular?

Is money sacred or secular? Is the beach sacred or secular? Is your automobile sacred or secular? Is your home secular or sacred? Are you secular or sacred?

Some like to think we determine which is which. But is that true? If the government passes laws or decrees labeling something as sacred or secular, does it make it so? Because your aunt tells you what is sacred, does it make it so? Or what your uncle believes makes it so?

What if I told you that everything is sacred because of who owns it and made it.

What makes something holy or secular is determined by its author. Whatever the Creator has made is an offshoot of His character. If the Creator is Holy, then His creation is holy.

But what happens when HIS original intent of purpose is changed without His approval? Then what is sacred may become polluted. In the eyes of an unbeliever, it becomes secular (separate from God's purpose). Yet, through God's eye, it is still redeemable. In God's eyes it is still holy. But the holiness is lost through man's eyes by his carnal desire to solely gratify himself.

For example, God created the earth. But mankind abuses the environment for his personal gain.

God created the social institutions of government, business, and education. But mankind disbar His authority for personal ambition and gain.

God created the sacredness of sex. But people pervert it for personal gain.

Everything God made and makes is holy and sacred. But whether we keep to His purpose and intent is the driving factor. It will determine whether its full purpose is being recognized and experienced.

So, we need to acknowledge the Triune God's authority in everything around us. Then stop separating everything between secular and sacred. Otherwise this wonderful world's potential will never be fully realized.

O yes, that is why we look forward to Jesus' return. When a new age begins. When HE leads governments to take part in His original plan for creation. Heaven on earth in its totality is coming!

#28 - Blessed How?

"Blessed be the God and Father of our Lord Jesus Christ, who has blessed us in Christ with every spiritual blessing in the heavenly places, even as he chose us in him before the foundation of the world, that we should be holy and blameless before him. In love he predestined us for adoption as sons through Jesus Christ, according to the purpose of his will, to the praise of his glorious grace, with which he has blessed us in the Beloved. In him we have redemption through his blood, the forgiveness of our trespasses, according to the riches of his grace, which he lavished upon us, in all wisdom and insight making known to us the mystery of his will, according to his purpose, which he set forth in Christ as a plan for the fullness of time, to unite all things in him, things in heaven and things on earth.
In him we have obtained an inheritance, having been predestined according to the purpose of him who works all things according to the counsel of his will, so that we who were the first to hope in Christ might be to the praise of his glory. In him you also, when you heard the word of truth, the gospel of your salvation, and believed in him, were sealed with the promised Holy Spirit, who is the guarantee of our inheritance until we acquire possession of it, to the praise of his glory."
Ephesians 1:3-14

Last week the question arose in regards to my email address that I use for solicitation purposes. In its name is an acronym for Blessed. So I was asked how am I blessed?

After I gave one of my smirk smiles and before I could answer, he began to ask: blessed with good health? Money? Family? Work? How are you blessed?

My reply? I am blessed with a trustful relationship with the Triune God. Anything that comes from that relationship is secondary. There is nothing better than being known and knowing the Creator God.

What compares?

He is the source, the reason, and purpose behind life. Everything is known by Him. He shares HIS life with me and others. HE allows me to share my life with HIM. He lets us play in his worldwide sandbox. He wants us to explore, discover, and learn from Him. Through the challenges of life, He wants us to lean on Him. To Trust Him as He navigates us through the redemption maze.

To know Him and to be known by Him in a favorite light is the greatest blessing one can receive in this life. What would it take for you to realize the same?

#29 - Through Faith or By Faith

"For by grace you have been saved through faith. And this is not your own doing; it is the gift of God, not a result of works, so that no one may boast". Eph 2:8-9

Faith is given to us by God. We don't generate faith. God disperses faith (Rm. 12:3). It is His gift to us. We either exercise it or not.

We exercise faith when we walk it out and through it. Faith is not the cause of our salvation. We are not saved by faith, but by grace. We are saved (justified) by the grace of Jesus Christ. But, by walking through the faith given to us, we are being saved (regenerated) into the image of Jesus Christ.

Poor theology places the cause of salvation with our faith. Our response is not the cause of salvation; our response is the effect of salvation. In the words of cause and effect, our salvation is caused by Jesus Christ. Our response is the effect of salvation.

If our faith is the cause of salvation, then we wouldn't need a savior. Yet, since Jesus Christ is the reality of salvation, we either accept that reality or not. When we accept that reality, we begin to experience the power of salvation.

A good example is gravity. We acknowledge its existence and respect its authority. Your belief doesn't cause gravity to exist. You acknowledge the truth and accordingly live life.

So walk your life through the faith God has given you. Be grateful for the grace He has bestowed upon you. There is nothing to boast about except what God has done.

Thus, learn to live out your life with the faith He has already given you. You will be surprised by the outcome.

#30 - Entitlement Theology

"...for the kingdom of God is not eating and drinking, but righteousness and peace and joy in the Holy Spirit." Romans 14:17 (NASB)

Good theology is life-giving. Poor theology is life-draining. Good theology is built upon the character of God. Poor theology is grounded in projected fantasy. Good theology is integrated within the good news of Jesus Christ. Poor theology is centered around human passions.

There are believers whose knowledge of God is flawed around the entitlement mindset. They generally have been exposed to a message that God's purpose is about you the individual. That your salvation is an agreement where God's purpose is to exchange his blessing for your loyalty. That His sole mission is for your success and happiness. That you are the center of the universe and He will make all your dreams and desires become reality.

If this is you, you may want to reread your Bible.

Take Jonah as an example. God called him with the mission to preach to the people of Nineveh, his enemies. Jonah instead chose to flee from God. God though in his mercy worked out circumstances for Jonah to change his mind. He eventually made it to Nineveh, preached, and the people repented. You would think that Jonah would have been delighted with the results. Instead he pouted. God's actions didn't align with his beliefs. He thought that God should have destroyed these people. But God had other plans.

Entitlement theology is centered around the self. Instead of making our story and goals the main purpose of life, we need to surrender to our Lord's purpose. When we do, the byproduct is to experience the richness of God's character. We still have our dreams and goals but have submitted these under the Lordship of Jesus Christ. Which means, if we are allowed to pursue and achieve them we are grateful and appreciative. Yet it also means if we are not allowed to achieve them, we are also grateful and appreciative.

Our life is hidden in Jesus Christ. His story is the main one. Our story is a very, very, very small byline within His storyline. Apart from Him, we would be on death row. He has introduced us to His Father who has adopted us into the divine family. Not because we are entitled, but because Jesus Christ is entitled to everything. He is the reason we live, breathe, and have hope today and tomorrow. And yes, we are included.

#31 – What Pleases God?

"And without faith it is impossible to please Him, for he who comes to God must believe that He is and that He is a rewarder of those who seek Him." NASB Hebrews 11:6

Some of my fellow brothers in the Lord seem to think one can please God without necessarily trusting Him. Others say no, God is pleased by only those who trust Him.

What does today's scripture state?

God's desire for man is to gain a full grasp of reality. To know what is good and evil from His perspective. To always behave in a Christlike manner which produces the best outcome for self and others. When our actions, words, and attitudes please God, they also have a positive impact on those around us.

As we learn to trust God, we submit ourselves to His purpose. Most of the time it may still involve the pursuit of our dreams and goals. But at times we may have to delay or even set aside our plans to fulfil His design for us. Even then, we know God has our best interest at heart. That under His grace, events and circumstances may or may not workout in this life. But if not, and if still desirable, in the new age.

As written, the key to pleasing God is our faith.

To the Hebrews, faith is an active word that involves action with belief. That belief is built upon walking out a trustful relationship with the Maker of life. In other words, faith is more than a mental exercise.

What about unbelievers who behave in a loving manner? Without knowing who God is, are you saying that God is not pleased? We are not anyone's judge. God is doing a work in each of us. Some HE is discipling in the faith. Others HE is soothing their hurts. Some HE is endowing them with physical riches. All HE is enriching with his Spirit. He is involved in everyone's life. The question though becomes who is involved in His?

Faith is a gift from Him. We are now learning how to exercise the faith we have been given. When we extend ourselves and lean on him, a mutual bonding relationship is developed. From this relationship, trust – a two-way process – is slowed put in place. This active trust is what pleases God. From this position, we can sacrifice everything and know He has our best intention at heart. That all things eventually work for good. Without this faith, it is impossible to please Him. But God in his universal grace has bestowed that faith with every one of us. We only need to accept His reality, unleash His potential in us, and learn to run with it.

#32 - Roux of God

"But thanks be to God, who always leads us in triumph in Christ, and manifests through us the sweet aroma of the knowledge of Him in every place." 2 Corinthians 2:14 (NASB)

Taking a mixture of fat and flour is a classic French thickening agent used for soups and sauces. The French word is "roux." Typically, one could also add other items into the mixture to bring out more flavor from your dish.

The same is true with God. As Paul wrote, the knowledge of Jesus Christ is manifested through God's children. He is liken to a pleasant fragrance. Our lives are like the pleasant smell of roux over one's meal. As we walk and live in Christ, His sweetness is manifested through our lives.

The roux of God comes from the Holy Spirit. The fruit of the Spirit is the natural character of God. When He made His abode with you, He gives you the opportunity to allow Him to express Himself through you. This is what happens when you deny yourself and yield to the working of the Holy Spirit. The natural byproduct is allowing the aroma of God to manifest itself from Him to you and from you to others.

This may not be the best analogy but is one way of drawing this picture. What God does in us and through us to touch the lives of others is like this.

God's roux – pleasant but effective. Challenging but rewarding. Awkward at times but refreshing to the soul. The roux of God is for those who choose to take part with Him in the life of the Triune circle.

#33 – Do You Fear Missing Out (FOMO)?

"And we know that God causes all things to work together for good to those who love God, to those who are called according to His purpose." Romans 8:28

Are you missing out on what God has for you?

Most likely if you are not attuned to God's purpose for life, you will have misplaced expectations. They could lead you into frustration and anger. Even though life is good, circumstances sometimes stink beyond measure. This is why if you only look through your physical accomplishments, you may miss God's intention for you.

God's long-term goal is to prepare you for eternity. You have been adopted into His family. His desire for you is to prepare you to rule and minister in the same manner Jesus Christ displayed while on earth. He wants you ready for greater service in the family business: The Kingdom of God.

Satan's big lie to Adam and Eve was to place doubt into their minds that God cannot be trusted. That God's plan denies one from experiencing life's good things. This is a lie that Satan still propagates throughout the world.

But God's grace is greater than Man's distorted expectations. The Holy Spirit has the knack to use stinking circumstances for our benefit. We often find ourselves encamped in spiritual quicksand. But HE produces fruit through the ordeal. HE is creating a spiritual masterpiece within us. HE impregnates us with a seed of heavenly riches. He does so to remind us that God is always with us and working through us.

God knows your needs and desires. He also knows your strengths and how to best display them in this world and next for His kingdom. He uniquely designed you for an eternal purpose. Sometime, we may have to lose everything we have and believe before we reach a place in life of real contentment. When we do, no matter what the circumstances, we will still experience Christ's peace and joy.

Meanwhile, we are all on a journey of faith. Learning to trust God in the large and small decisions of life. Overtime, we will know that God has the best intentions in heart for you and me. Whether we experience our hearts desires in this world is no longer the issue. We know whatever we think we may miss out in this age, awaits us in the new age to come.

#34 - The Imaginary God

"This is eternal life, that they may know You, the only true God, and Jesus Christ whom You have sent." John 17:3

There was a game show back in the 1960s called "To Tell the Truth". A panel of four known celebrities would try to identify the real Mccoy. They would question each one of the three contestants to identify the real person. The other two imposters could lie, act, and do whatever to confuse the panelists. But the real character had to always tell the truth.

In many ways our search for the real God is like that game show. Growing up we read or hear stories about God but struggle with identifying who the real One is. Over time, some of us may even become so delusional with Him, we quit trying and join the agnostic team. Yet through diligence and patience, we slowly discover more about the real God as we pursue Him (James 4:8).

For many of us there is a battle in our minds trying to figure out this God. Depending on our upbringing, most of us as adults will have to relearn and rethink our brains. Then we will need to repent of our former image of God. When comparing the Triune God (Father, Son, Spirit) with the lone ranger god, our minds explode. The excess thought patterns become overwhelming. Most of us have not exercised our minds to handle such an inflow of information.

But God has made it easy for us to recognize Him. You come to know Him not only through creation, but in the person of Jesus Christ (Colossians 1:15). When we study the life of Jesus, accept His teachings, and follow Him, we come to know what He stated in John 14:20-23. You will experience life with the real God.

The same God that Jesus called Father is the same God you can come to know. The same Holy Spirit that Jesus called the Comforter, is the same Spirit you can come to know. And the same Jesus, who Father God stated He was well-pleased with (Matt. 3:17), is the same Jesus you can come to know.

Don't settle for an illusion. Don't take the words from others. But instead do your own homework. Seek out the one true Triune God who Jesus made known throughout His ministry. Your life will never be the same again.

#35 – Living Faith

"For just as the body without the spirit is dead, so also faith without works is dead." James 2:26

What is faith?

Faith is obedient action with trustful confidence in God's character. It is the confident assurance that God is always working out the best solution for you and others.

Any problem with Faith is typically tied to our ignorance of God. We believe what others have told us about God rather than discovering Him ourselves. We project our dysfunctional souls toward God, rather than believe Him and His Word.

We don't realize where we actually stand in His eyes. If we did, we would humbly and respectfully place all our being onto Him without concern with the outcome.

What is not faith?

Faith is not the inner belief of an outward expectation. Rather it is knowing Him with no concern with the results.

Faith is not the cause of your salvation. Rather it is the umbilical cord which connects you with the living Source of Life.

Faith is also not the anecdote of your situation. God is. Faith is your worldview of God's presence in the world and your role in His kingdom.

A living Faith is not only about moving mountains. But more so about healing your soul while serving others.

Through the graceful act of redemption and sanctification, you are being morphed. You are being molded after the image of Jesus Christ. A byproduct of this living faith is a more active soul. The fire within the deepest, inner workings of your soul is becoming more Godlike. It is a life not of empty motions but actions covered with inner joy. This outer behavior is a byproduct of the inner construct of a new creation. The work is being conducted by the Holy Spirit with your yielding cooperation.

This living faith is active, confident, and obedient to the Word and Spirit of God. It is built on God's viewpoint and not ours. The faith we trust in is not from us but is Christ's own faith. God's purpose for your life is a new creation according to His design. The process involves His Spirit developing His character in you. He is implanting HIS eternal values and divine love in you with all you speak, think, and do.

If this faith is not alive in you yet, pray and ask your heavenly Father to open your eyes to know Him better. Pursue Him with all your heart. In the process, over time, Christ's faith will become more perceptive and active. You will come to know Him and the workings of real, living faith. His faith will become your faith.

#36 - Enjoy Life in God's Presence

"Here is what I have seen to be good and fitting: to eat, to drink and enjoy oneself in all one's labor in which he toils under the sun during the few years of his life which God has given him; for this is his reward. Furthermore, as for every man to whom God has given riches and wealth, He has also empowered him to eat from them and to receive his reward and rejoice in his labor; this is the gift of God. For he will not often consider the years of his life, because God keeps him occupied with the gladness of his heart." Ecclesiastes 5:18-20 (NASB)

Ever notice when you are involved in an enjoyable project, time seems to move fast. Whether you are playing a video game, or watching an action-packed movie, the time goes by quick.

If you have an occupation that exercises your gifts, values, and passion, the day likewise flies by. Rather than be exhausted at the end of the day, you feel refresh and can't wait for tomorrow to start the work again. These activities are God's gift to you.

As the writer of Ecclesiastes states, whether you are a believer or not, doesn't matter. God has given people the gift of enjoyment. In fact, in our everyday life, He even includes our job. The sad outcome though is many people turn their work into their savior and lose out on all God's blessings. This is why one needs to find enjoy with God's creation plus always act and behave living in God's presence.

The joy of living life in God's presence is waking tomorrow without any regrets or penalties. There is great liberty when one learns to enjoy the natural everyday gifts God has bestowed upon us. We are blessed to have Him share His life with us and us with Him.

When life passes you by quickly, consider it God's gift to you. When you are in the final season of your time on earth, you can also thank God for occupying your heart with joy. For you will look back in all your work, play, and relationships, and realize HE has been very good to you. It's a nice place to be.

#37 - Discover God in Your Brokenness

"The Lord is near to the brokenhearted and saves those who are crushed in spirit." Psalms 34:18

The one place many of us discover the real God comes through our brokenness. Those times when we find ourselves at the end of our rope hanging on for dear life. The times we are at the bottom of the barrel with nowhere else to go. Those times when we suffered a great financial or relationship loss. Those times we don't know what to do next. God gracefully and timely (not my way or schedule) answers our prayer. It is from these experiences we learn ASAP - always stop and pray.

In my own walk, God became real in those unpleasant times. For me especially during those times of unemployment. It was between jobs where I didn't know how we were going to make the mortgage payment and put food on the table. It was these times when the answer from our prayer for daily bread became real. Thereafter, it became a family adventure to pray and watch. To observe how God was going to help us get out of this mess and other difficult situations.

As you read many of the classics of yesterday, you discover how saints discovered God. HIS gracefulness came alive during the difficult times of their lives. It seems most of us are too busy when times are good to see God's presence in a situation. But when times are bad is another story. After we have exhausted all our resources. When there is nothing else we can physically turn to, God makes His appearance. (Though He is always already there).

It is typically during these broken times we discover who God is. When we come to appreciate knowing He truly cares for us. So, the next time you find yourself busted, broken, and beaten, stop and don't rush through the process. Instead take time to develop the most important relationship on planet earth. He will reveal Himself to you when you seek Him. And when we are broken, there are not too many distractions to prevent us from getting to know Him better.

#38 – Number One Sinner

"Here is a trustworthy saying that deserves full acceptance: Christ Jesus came into the world to save sinners—of whom I am the worst. But for that very reason I was shown mercy so that in me, the worst of sinners, Christ Jesus might display his immense patience as an example for those who would believe in him and receive eternal life." 1 Timothy 1:15 (NIV)

When we compare ourselves with our neighbors, beware. When our perception is we are better then they, beware the blindness! It is always easier to see the speck in our neighbor's eye rather than the plank that is sticking through ours (Matt.7:5).

Yes, we need to recognize sin and its ugly consequences. When we approach our neighbors from a self-righteous attitude, alarm bells should ring. We are only setting ourselves up for a humpy-dumpty fall.

How did the apostle Paul keep himself grounded? He realized and knew he was the worst sinner of everyone. Yes, he no longer went about persecuting those who didn't believe as he did. But like the reformed alcoholic, he knew he was one drink away from collapse. One thought or action from being led down a path of unwavering slavery to its addiction.

His answers always pointed to Jesus Christ.

Because Jesus fulfilled HIS plan of redemption for humanity, Paul realized the change. His attitude and behavior was the result of the Spirit's work in him. Paul didn't take the accolades but gave them to whom it belong too – Jesus Christ. He was Christ's workmanship. The good works, the letters, the words, and the final product was only because of God's patience. HIS mercy. HIS love toward him and others.

So, like how D. T. Niles stated "evangelism is just one beggar telling another beggar where to find bread." So relationships are likewise built by one sinner telling another sinner. Reminding each of us where to find a real, long term solution.

#39 - Measuring Your Self-Worth

"God created man in His own image, in the image of God He created him; male and female He created them." Genesis 1:27 (NASB)

How do you measure yourself? What standard do you use? What is the basis of your value?

For many people, their success in life is measured by their accomplishments. Their achievements may include: Independent wealth. Political fame. Functional family. Educational credentials. Industry recognition. The list is endless.

For some though, they have come to a new realization. That all one's lifetime achievements combined together is vapor blowing into the wind. (Eccl. 1:2). Our real worth lies in Jesus Christ.

Being made in the image of God himself, humanity has a unique standing. Our value is not because of what or who we are, but because of who created us. Humanity's value is determined by God himself. He created us. He bestowed the gifts and abilities we possess. He birthed us in such a time as this. He is lovingly disciplining and encouraging us as we journey through life.

Being redeemed by Christ, you and I have been purchased from Satan's bondage. We have been ushered into God's royal chamber. You and I are God's children being prepared for leadership and ministry (Rev. 5:10). All because of the work of Jesus Christ.

We are His workmanship being prepared for good works (Eph.2:10). Thus, every person has value and deserves respect and honor. Our value is not determined by what we contribute to the whole. Instead our worth is measured by God's faithfulness for us.

God loves us so much He gave us Himself in Jesus Christ. In Christ, God was reconciling the world to himself (Col. 1:20). Through Christ, we have a direct relationship with the Creator. Everything was made by Christ through Christ for Christ (Col.1:16) who shares everything with us.

You are valuable in Christ. You are highly esteemed in Christ. You are very important in Christ. Your value lies in Christ. You are worth more than you truly realize. But only because of Jesus Christ.

#40 - Thirty is the Number

"Let your fountain be blessed and rejoice in the wife of your youth." Proverbs 5:18

The Bible showcases the significance of the number thirty. I give credit to Rabbi Dr. Hillel ben David for these points. They include:

- Thirty represents reconciliation at a higher level
- Thirty was the age of strength
- Thirty was the age one began their mission
- Thirty days is a period of mourning for someone special
- Thirty days is the totality of the moon's lunar cycle
- Thirty is a time of transition

Whatever the significance of thirty may or may not represent, there is a lesson for us married men. The lesson is to invest in our marriage relationship every day. In today's, fast paced, convenient culture, time to build up each other gets lost in the daily grind. Sometimes, if not most the time, we give relationship building the second fiddle. So, one good game plan to put in place each day is take the number 'thirty' to a whole higher level.

What if we would invest at least thirty-minutes of prayer time each day with our Lord? What if we allocated the time to have a thirty-minute one-on-one talk with our spouse? What if we included a thirty-second hug with her each day? What impact would have to keep your marriage alive and strong for the long term?

We all get busy at times and usually our relationships suffer. This may be a simple method for those of us who are super active. This may be a way to develop the discipline to make time for the real important people in life. It has worked wonders for over thirty-five years with my marriage. And I'm sure it will for you.

#41 - Which is the More Prudent Choice?

"If any of you lacks wisdom, let him ask God, who gives generously to all without reproach, and it will be given him." James 1:5

What is the basis of your decision? When you have a choice to make, how much weight do you focus on the outcome? Is the basis of your decision dollars or righteousness? Do you involved God in the beginning of the process or simply ask Him to bless your final choice?

When confronted with multiple choices which is the best one?

Decisions are often based on the values you consider most important. For most of us, our values are formed early in our childhood. We didn't put a request of which values we wanted. They simple all arrived one day in a bundled package. That is after years of being formed in you without your consent. Then begins a lifelong process of evaluating and modifying your values. But how do you know the values you choose are the best ones for you?

Now you may have discovered a different reason for studying the Bible. Within the pages of this Book, are gems of long standing proven values. Values which have generated positive and negative results. The Book is a historic compilation of defining what is good for humanity. It also showcases what produces pain for the long term.

Sin may be a Biblical term. But sin outlines which values destroy relationships and prevents people from flourishing. God's character on the other hand, demonstrates what values produce Shalom. Human flourishing, blessedness, and Shalom are key outcomes of making choices. These results are built on the eternal values of the Creator God.

When you begin to get this knowledge. When you gain understanding of its implications. Then apply these treasures in your life, you find God's grace and generosity wherever you go. You begin to act from a position of confidence. You discover the real values which life fruitfully grows from with more than enough.

These values are the seeds of choice. When decisions are built upon the eternal values of God, you are walking in alignment with HIS design. You are living life within HIS intrinsic character strength. You begin to view life and outcomes for the long term. Not only for yourself but for the benefit of the entire community. Your choices and decisions become godlike.

It all begins by acknowledging HIM. Accepting HIM. And yielding to HIS involvement in your life. Ask HIM.

#42 - Perception

"For the heart of this people has become dull, with their ears they scarcely hear, and they have closed their eyes, otherwise they would see with their eyes, hear with their ears, and understand with their heart and return, and I would heal them.'" Matt. 13:15 (NASB)

The other day there was money to be made trading the futures market. The volatility was lively and volume at extreme highs. Yet at the end of the day I didn't even make one entry. As I reviewed the day's activity, the realization of my perceived blindness shocked me.

I spent the day seeking out one setup that has been very good for me during times of volatility. The setup this day never happened. Yet, in review I notice five other types of entries that I have successful profited in the past. Yet this day, I was blind to these opportunities.

Lesson learned.

How often do we walk through the day focused on one specific outcome? And ignore all other opportunities?

Our perception is not reality. Today there was real money made by those who were open to different possibilities. My perception never occurred. thus, I didn't profit from the day. Yet the fact is money was made by many others. Their perception aligned with what was truly happening that day.

When it comes to God, our perception is either align with Him or not. Ignorance blinds us from seeing or hearing what is actually happening. A narrow mind focused on a perceived idea may limit one from what is actually happening. A misunderstood word may blind one from what is actually happening. A dull ear may also limit one from knowing what is actually happening.

But an open mind, heart, eye, and ear seeks the truth from all sources. Instead of viewing the situation from one single view, we need to be mindful. We need to be open to other possibilities. We need confirmation from reality.

Whether trading the market or walking with our Father, our perception is limited. Yet when we are open-minded. When we realize there is more before us than we see and hear. Then maybe we can begin to discover what is really happening before us.

Perception is not reality, but only one person's opinion. Don't confuse opinion with reality.

#43 – Re-Do

"...but where sin increased, grace abounded all the more..." Romans 5:20 (NASB)

There is more grace than sin available for your life (Romans 5 & 6). Just as God is greater than any sin, His grace is also always more than whatever sin enslaves you. Not that you deliberately choose to sin and abuse His grace. But when we disappointingly fail for the umpteen time, HIS grace is more than enough for you to try again.

For God's grace corners the market on do-overs and second chances. HE grants us the opportunity to try again, and again, and again. Again. Again. Again. Again. Again. Again. Again. Again. etc.

Life is a learning process preparing you and I for eternity. Do-overs are a part of the process of growth. Like every professional endeavor it requires time and diligent effort to master. So does discipleship.

For example, Peter denied Jesus three times. But Jesus poured out his grace upon him on the beach. Peter thereafter spoke boldly His name wherever he went.

When Saul the Jewish persecutor of Christians was knocked off his high horse. Jesus confronted him. HE redirected his life mission to serving Christ rather than fighting him.

During our life journey, we will likewise be knocked down. Rugs pulled from under us. Lied too. Gossiped about. Reputation driven through the mud. Fired. Beaten. Misunderstood. Put our foot in our mouth. Kicked from behind. Succumb to our addictions. Introduced to new vices. This is only the start of the list. Through all this, you can be assured our heavenly Father still loves you. HE will continue to pour out His grace upon you.

He has promised He will complete the work He has started in you.

You only have to keep trying again, and again, and again...He will do the rest.

#44 – Be a Blessing

"I will make you into a great nation, and I will bless you; I will make your name great, and you will be a blessing." Genesis 12:2 (NIV)

You were created to be a blessing for God and others! think of Abraham. He was blessed by God as His chosen vessel to fulfill His plans for humanity. God has also chosen and blessed you to be a blessing for others.

Many of us spend most of our lives seeking to be blessed. We want God's favor. We want riches, relationships, and respect. We want. We want. We want. Yet somewhere in our journey we will meet up with our true self. Then we will come to realize what a blind, ignorant, self-centered creature we have been.

We will eventually repent of our attitude and behavior. We will then begin to better hear God's truth as He unfolds our story with His and begins to renovate our heart. The end result is a new creation patterned after Jesus Christ.

So why fight it any longer?

The sooner we come to realize we are all walking down a path to death's doorway. This dilemma will make us realize what Paul wrote about in 1 Corinthians 15:26. The #1 enemy of all humanity is death.

But the #1 solution has already arrived. His name is Jesus. He resolved our dilemma by living a perfect life and offering His life in exchange for ours. In the process He opened the door for us to begin exploring eternity.

When the realization hits you that God has a universal eternal plan. That HIS plan already includes you, me, and our neighbors. Our typical response is "how do I join?"

When you join Him in His walk, He rubs off on you. His Character, Attitude, and Values become yours. You begin to see life through His eyes. You heart opens up for the success of others. You find ways to contribute your talents, gifts, and treasures for the sake of others.

You come to realize you were created to be a blessing for God and others. Wherever you walk with God, you seek ways to uplift others. You restore those who have been broken. You introduce everyone to the One who is the Center of Life. He is the source of everything good, the truth, and the way.

In other words, since you were created to be a blessing, who will you bless today?

#45 – Pray. Listen. Do.

...Everyone who is of the truth listens to my (Jesus) voice." John 18:37

When a crisis occurs in your life, how do you react? When you are at the end of your rope for solutions, where do you turn to? When no one seems to understand you or care, where do you go for support?

We are all human with similar needs, desires, and responses. How we react to adverse situations over time is typically a byproduct of a learned response. Whether we have a violent temper or a foul mouth tongue. Whether we have a beaten-up self-image, or overly self-confident. There are multiple responses as there are people.

But one response has proven over and over again to work most effective when given the chance. This is when one turns the matter over to our Creator. From there we watch how He reveals His love and care for us. Then we learn the power of praying, listening, and doing.

The Kingdom of God operates through the heart of its citizens. Unless one is in contact with the Lord of the House, one doesn't reap the benefits. One needs to have a personal relationship with the King. When you have the King's ear, you have someone who can make the difference in everything you do. So, when you learn to listen and do what your King suggests, you have a very good source of knowing what is best. So stop your busyness. Explore all the other possibilities you haven't considered.

Most of us start with the doing phase. We focus on what must we do. Instead our focus needs to be on leaning more on Him through prayer. And in our prayer, we need to spend more time listening than speaking. The Spirit already knows the best solution for your dilemma. We only have to learn to pray, listen, and then do.

#46 – Steward Well

"His master said to him, 'Well done, good and faithful servant. You were faithful with a few things; I will put you in charge of many things; enter into the joy of your master.'" Matt. 25:21

Do you want to serve in a great ministry? Then start right where you are at. Your ministry will become great when you focus on the smaller details of God's Kingdom.

He has given you the responsibility to steward the resources at your disposal. You say you have only very little? That is OK; steward well. You are from a small family with few relational connections? That is OK; steward well. You have no job? That is OK; steward well. You have a physical disability? That is OK; steward well. No matter how much or how little you have; start today and steward well with what you have at your disposal.

We all manage the resources we hold for greatest impact. Most of us are still trying to hoard what little we have instead of sharing it with others. Somewhere we still believe the pie is limited. We don't really understand God's Kingdom economics. We forget Jesus multiplied the five loafs of bread and two fish to feed at least 5,000 people. We have trouble believing it can be done again with the resources at our disposal.

For to steward well is to trust God.

When you come to understand everything is own by God, you will see a different world. You will understand HE has given you what you have to manage it with Him. You now hold yourself accountable to Him. You first seek His purpose before succumbing to your desires. You (and sometimes reluctantly) follow through with His instructions for you. Over time, you learn that He provides as we learn to trust Him and walk with Him.

For most of us, our faith will be tested through the "small things" in life. Yes, it is through the small and routine avenues of life where our strength is developed. Where our trust in God becomes real. So that when the "big one comes", we will only do what we have done our entire life – trust God and steward well.

#47 - More Than You Expect

"Now to Him who is able to do far more abundantly beyond all that we ask or think, according to the power that works within us..." Ephesians 3:20 NASB.

Sometimes I stop and look back at the last forty years of life and shake my head in disbelief. How I failed to trust God in the difficult circumstances of everyday living bewilders me. I believed in God most of my entire life but did not believe Him until the second half of living. Again, if I could have, I would have. But life is a learning experience preparing us for eternity.

If I could reset time, there would be a few areas of life I would change. One area would be to remove the limitations I placed on God and myself.

I knew about God's love, but how much HE loved me was an issue. I didn't know we are one of God's favorites. My inaccurate attitude was He constantly tested me for personal pleasure. He would allow me to be thrown into situations that would take my breath away. He would allow circumstances that would cause severe financial hardship. I didn't receive blessings from Him (I mistakenly believed), but pain and sorrow.

Now in hindsight, I realize how much He cared for me. HE protectively allowed me to go through trials, circumstances, and challenges. The purpose was to strengthen me and learn to trust Him. I've also came to realize how many limitations we place on ourselves because we limit Him.

The more we came to lean on Him, the more we trusted Him. The more we partnered with Him, the more He revealed Himself to me. Not with his physical Presence. But through the people, events, and circumstances of life – through His Creation.

Today, I am more amazed at how He works through others to reveal His blessings. The way He brings people into your life. The way He works out circumstances to bring about events which speaks to you. The way He gives you the strength and courage to seek out the best.

Everything is possible with Him. He knows what is best for you. Yes, you and I have limitations. But God has no limits. He is eternal. He is omnipresent. He made a commitment with you at creation. We only have to accept His authority in our life and get out of His way.

He is always going before you. Talk with Him. Ask Him how you can best present yourself to others. Trust Him. Lean on Him. He is doing a work in you for His glory, not yours. When you surrender to His goals and objectives, you allow Him to work through you.

The result is a manifestation of His greatness. Your talents which He endowed you with plus the skills you develop are join together for His purpose. This plus His love for you opens doors beyond one's expectations. Together you will see more what He has in mind for you. And you will come to realize He has more in store for you than you can ever think, ask, or imagine.

#48 - What Do You Mean by That?

"Blessed is the one who finds wisdom, and the one who gets understanding..." Proverbs 3:13

One of the biggest challenges we all face is effectively communicating with others. As we speak with others, the ability to understand is imperative. The skill to be understood is also highly desired by many in the leadership world.

Johnson O'Connor Research team has conducted studies of thousands of CEOs. They have identified their highest ranking skill is the ability to communicate. Even in marriage, this skill is important. The struggle between two people unable to communicate their feelings/emotions is common. It is one of the largest complaints for divorce and separation.

One key point for effective communications is better understanding. To understand the other person before trying to explain your position is a game changer. How many times do we make assumptions that later proved incorrect? What if we first clarified the definition of certain words? Wouldn't we find ourselves more effective in speaking and writing?

Among my fellow siblings in the Lord, I always try to clarify the meaning of certain phrases and words. You ever notice how many buzz words are used within the Christian culture? Take for example words like faith. grace. incarnation. salvation. kingdom of God. Trinity. These and many more are used interchangeably with a different meaning among us. So before answering or jumping to conclusion, we need common understanding. At times I have found it necessary to draw word pictures or stories to clarify the definition of one word.

Now I am not an English major, nor a word smith. But I know enough that the purpose of words is to communicate a concept or thought. So, I don't get bent out of shape when words may be poorly used. As long as we both are looking at the same big picture meaning.

One simple tool to clarify how the speaker is using a word is to ask, "what do you mean by that?" The more both sides have a clearer picture of what is being discussed, the easier to find a meeting of the minds.

So, like Proverbs 3:13 states, you will find yourself blessed when you first get understanding. Then the wisdom to apply it. It all begins when you ask, "what do you mean by that?"

#49 - Symptom or Problem?

"Woe to you, scribes and Pharisees, hypocrites! For you clean the outside of the cup and of the dish, but inside they are full of robbery and self-indulgence." NASB.

Many in the Church today focus on outward behavior rather than the matter of the heart. By heart, we mean the soul. The emotional, thinking, value-center operating system which makes you, you.

We point to Adam and Eve who committed the first human sin. For most people that sin was disobedience toward God. Yet, my argument is the sin was committed even before then. For the outward behavior of sin is really the result of a deeper inner problem.

The real sin was separating oneself from God. Instead of leaning on Him and partnering with Him, Eve began a relationship with the Serpent. It was the Serpent who came between God and Eve. He came to divide and lead one astray from the Center of Life. He does the same today.

Sin occurs even before the behavioral act is displayed. Jesus himself throughout the Gospel books emphasized the heart of the matter. Not just the physical act itself. The outward act is only the symptom of an inner problem. The problem is a heart empty of God's presence.

For it is from the Holy Spirit living within you that strengthens you. The Spirit coaches you and leads you away from destructive behavior. Jesus was born by and with the Holy Spirit from the beginning of his earthly life. For the rest of us, we allow the Spirit to enter into our inner self only after we have accepted His authority in our life. The Bible identifies this as being born again.

Jesus also refers to the Kingdom of God beginning from within you. When the Spirit is married with your spirit, you learn to cooperate together. You find the inner attitude and confidence to handle temptation. You exercise the same faith Jesus employed against Satan in his wilderness temptation.

You also begin to experience life dancing with the Almighty. You live in His presence through your daily routines. Life becomes more than judging each other's outer performance. Instead, it becomes life in the Spirit preparing you for eternity. You are being trained to be more effective in your work, relationships, and struggles. The end result is God being glorified through your actions.

So, don't focus on the symptom. Rather identify the problem. You will then arrive at a better solution to move you toward your objectives.

#50 – Love and Respect

"Love each other devotedly and with brotherly love; and set examples for each other in showing respect." Romans 12:10 (CJB)

There are relationship principles taught throughout the Bible. When practiced makes the Kingdom of God come alive. One such principle is the relationship between leaders and followers. This would apply in business, government, and yes even the little-league baseball game.

This principle is built around the concept of love and respect. Both attributes are necessary for a healthy relationship between two parties. When practiced the relationship is fully engaged. In summary, the follower is to respect the authority of the leader and the leader is to love the follower. What does this look like in a practical setting?

In the home, the Bible teaches that the husband is to love his wife as Christ loves the Church (Eph 5:25). Which means he is willing to sacrifice his life (time, money, possessions, goals, body, etc.) for her. On the other side, the wife is to respect (show honor) for her husband. Both sides are to mutually submit one to another (Eph. 5:21).

In the workplace, bosses are to care for their employees as unto the Lord (Col.4:1). The employees are to serve their leaders as serving Jesus Christ (Eph.6:5). Love and respect show up again.

In government, we are instructed to honor the emperor (I Pt.2:17). The king is to operate from a position of steadfast love and faithfulness (Proverb 20:28). Again, love and respect show their power.

What if the other side doesn't cooperate in the relationship? Simple answer: You do your part and let the Lord do His. We pray and ask our heavenly Father to shower His grace upon them. Since He has shared His grace upon us, don't we want all to experience the same joy?

I'm sure we don't have to be selfish with Him. He has so much more to share with others; and isn't it exciting to watch how He invades the lives of others? You will find during your life travels that much grace is going to be handed out toward others. Many who may not understand the ways of God. You may be the prayer warrior who introduces our Rabbi to them. So, let love and respect find their way into your relationships. Then see how the kingdom of God comes alive in your world.

#51 – God's Will

"The Lord has established His throne in the heavens,
And His sovereignty rules over all." Psalms 103:19 (NASB)

What is God's Will for your life?

One process to follow is to understand how the Bible presents His Will. In summary format, you could classify His Will into three dimensions. Providential. Moral. Personal.

Providential is God's invisible hand leading history as He desires. A good example is the prophecy and fulfillment of Israel and Jesus Christ. From the beginning of time God had specified plans which he foretold. Then HE worked them out through various people, tribes, and nations.

God's Moral Will is the basis of how we relate with one another. His Will is a byproduct of His character. The Ten Commandments reveal His heart. All the other principles throughout Scripture are the outward focus of His love. Jesus himself stated that to love God and care for our neighbors is the fulfillment of His love. As we practice His love, we are in His Will.

God's Personal Will for you is the one we most likely mean when we seek His Will for our life. This is aligning yourself with the talents and gifts HE empowered you with. This along with discovering your place in the Body of Christ opens the pathway for your destiny. It is having a personal relationship with our Creator. It is knowing the Triune God and making Him known before others.

So, what is God's Will for your life?

For most of us, God's Will is not a global ministry but a personal crusade. God may choose you for a specific long-term mission, but for most of us they are short term assignments. It is to know Him and make Him and His ways known. As we live in His Presence, He shares His life with us and we share His life with others, we are in His Will.

So when we come to a fork in life's journey and seek direction, most of us get stuck. We think there is only one solution or one direction that is God's way and everything else is not. Eventually we may learn the fork in the road is to exercise the wisdom He has bestowed upon us. It is to seek wise counsel from those who may have been there before. It is to pray and seek insight from the Lord. HE knows your talents, skills, and the real opportunities before you.

This is but a moment for you to mature in wisdom and judgement.

When you realize your God is always with you no matter which road you choose, you walk in confidence. The outcome will be OK. In hindsight it may not have been the best decision, but if you could have none differently, you would have. But based on the information you collected; you made the best choice you knew.

God's Will is wider and deeper and more opportunistic then many of us allow. We place limited boundaries upon God. Remember, HE does the impossible. Those of us whose faith is yet maturing, HE prunes.

So, don't limit yourself. God is for you. His Will for you is to know Him. To make Him known to others. To build relationships with one another. As you mature and grow in the faith, you will find you are in His Will most of the time.

#52 – Glorify God

"I give thanks to you, O Lord my God, with my whole heart, and I will glorify your name forever."
Psalms 86:12

"...and call upon me in the day of trouble; I will deliver you, and you shall glorify me." Psalms 50:15

This morning I had the joy of biking for twelve miles against a warm, steady and strong, southwestern wind. With the wind behind pushing me forward, I felt like an eagle souring through the sky. But with the wind blowing in front of me, it felt like climbing a 30-degree steep hill. In both directions, it made me think what life is like living with God versus against Him.

When we align ourselves with the Author of Reality, life is like the wind behind us. We find strength we didn't know we had. We move forward toward our destination and goals with ease. With very little effort, and often while resting, our objectives unfold before us.

But when we fight against the Truth, we are constantly fighting a battle against the wind. We have to increase our energy level. Our legs, arms, and body hurts from the excessive work we have to put in. Even when we reach our destination, we are tired and beaten from the experience. The joy of the journey turns into a fiasco of pain.

Yes, there are days when our world is turned upside down. Yet life upside down with God is more manageable than life upside down and rebelling against Him.

When we made up our mind to stop fighting the Truth and accepted the reality of Jesus Christ's work, things changed. We found ourselves on our knees praising HIM. With arms lifted up we thanked and praised Father–Son–Spirit.

When we realized He wants to share His life with us, we were overcome with amazement. When HE allows us to live in His Presence, how can we not rejoice? When we became aware HE made everything so you and I could enjoy life with Him, how can we not stop and glorify Him?

We are grateful for the life he has given us. We appreciate the opportunities He provides us to grow and mature. We are thankful to live in such a time as this in history. How can we not stop and give Him the glory He alone deserves?

We are appreciative for leading us to discover our natural talents and gifts-the DNA He has uniquely equipped us with. As we allow Him to direct our steps toward serving others, we find fulfilment. The longer we walk with him the greater becomes the meaning and purpose for living. The result is a fruitful and quality improvement of our life. All which also enhances the life of those who we love and serve. How can we not stop and give Him the glory He alone deserves?

We are at awe to realize this sandbox, called Earth, was made for us to work and play in. That He has given us instructions how to make life more enjoyable for each of us. How can we not stop and give Him the glory He alone deserves?

As we become familiar with His story, we are honored to walk with HIM in HIS script. As HE invites us to take part with Him in playing out our role, we are humbled. To know HE will grant us eternity with HIM is mind blowing. How can we not stop and give Him the glory He alone deserves?

Everything was made through and for Jesus Christ. And as the gospel reveals, He includes you and me with Him. He shares his throne with us. He also shares His righteousness. And HE shares everything else because He loves us and wants what is best for us. How can we not stop and give Him the glory He alone deserves?

He is the center of our life. Everything flows from Him and through us and into each other. How can we not stop and give Him the glory He alone deserves?

Bottom-line: whenever, whatever, and wherever, always take time to stop and give Him the glory He deserves.

#53 – Live Well

"...so that you may live a life worthy of the Lord and please him in every way: bearing fruit in every good work, growing in the knowledge of God..." Colossians 1:10

What happens when life is measured by one's possessions, status, bank account, or influence? One has become swallowed up by the demon of pride – mankind's #1 vice. The focus is on self rather than God which leads to missing out on His best. But when our Heavenly Father is the center of life, one experiences His soulful riches. He provides the best of both worlds. His kingdom treasures along with the physical necessities of creation.

So, do you want to live well? To the fullest of your potential? With meaning and purpose? Then you need to know God better than you know yourself. For the fact is:

You live well when you partner with God while you travel through time and space. You will discover who you are. You will unleash your God-given talents. You will fulfill your divine purpose.

You live well when you take the cards you have been dealt with and play to win. Without excuses, self-pity, or shifting blame toward others.

You live well when character becomes more important than money. When your attitude is more valuable than muscle. When love is more fulfilling than intelligence.

You live well when wisdom replaces stupidity. When grace supersedes tolerance. When godliness displaces humanism.

You live well when work is your ministry. When your family is your sanctuary. When your neighbors are the doorway to experience God's love.

You live well when your word is your commitment. When your integrity is your suit or dress for the day. When your primary concern is for the welfare of others.

You live well when you accept the season of your life. When you are grateful for your state of health (no matter how broken you are). When you walk in hope even though you are unsure of the future.

You live well by being generous with your time and money. When you speak softly with those who disrespect you. When you are slow to anger by those who want to harm you.

You live well when you do good wherever you are. When you are fruitful in whatever your hand finds to do. When you gladly glorify God who made you and allowed you to live in such a time as this.

You truly live well when you have totally surrendered to the King of Kings and Lord of Lords. When you make His Kingdom your #1 daily priority each day.

You live well when you are true to yourself. When you are transparent in your relationships. When you add value without fanfare with others.

You live well when you serve along Jesus Christ. When you know HE holds you in His Grip since redeeming you before you even knew him.

You live well when you learn to quickly forgive yourself. When you extend the same forgiveness toward others. When you trust God to remedy the situation.

You live well by learning more about the Author of Life. When you let His Story unfold each day. When you partner within His Plans.

In other words, living life to the fullest, rooted in Jesus Christ, is to live well.

#54 - Be Fruitful

"And God blessed them. And God said to them, "Be fruitful and multiply and fill the earth and subdue it..." Genesis 1:28

"...we have not ceased to pray for you, asking that you may be filled with the knowledge of his will in all spiritual wisdom and understanding, so as to walk in a manner worthy of the Lord, fully pleasing to him: bearing fruit in every good work and increasing in the knowledge of God..." Colossians 1:9-10

God's first instructions to mankind taken from Genesis 1:28 was to "Be fruitful and multiply and fill the earth and subdue it..." Nothing has changed since then. Especially humanity's natural inclination to first try it their way.

At the very beginning our heavenly Father gave us personal responsibility. We are to exercise wisdom, imagination and creativity to manage His earthly domain. The Bible calls it stewardship.

We are like the manager of a company given the responsibility to grow the business for the owner. We have been given the assignment to improve the world around us. When we take the focus away from ourselves and on others, we find needs to be satisfied. Problems to be solved.

As a steward, we analyze the resources at our disposal. We deploy them toward satisfying the needs of others. In business, we receive a reward of developing a relationship with our customer. Through this process, we are compensated. This allows us to buy more resources and do it again. As we keep repeating the process, our client base grows. Our resources under management grows. The more people we serve, the larger our influence becomes.

The challenge for most of us is locating the sweet spot where our talents intersect the needs of others. Some of us may not recognize what our strengths are. Others have placed mental or emotional limits on themselves. Then others are so wrapped up in themselves that they are blind to the need of others.

The apostle Paul's letter to the Colossians refers to his prayer for them. He asks God to supply them with strength to walk with our Lord and be fruitful in their work. Do you think some of us (if not all) need to invest more time praying for the same resources?

Is it possible we are not as fruitful as we can be because we are trying to accomplish our dreams apart from God? Instead of striving for more, working longer hours, and chasing after dollars, ask Him to show us how to rest in Him. To learn from Him how to be more fruitful. Most of us will become surprised how He has a way to open doors. To bring people into your world, and generate opportunities beyond our wildest imagination.

God wants you to be fruitful in your work. But more than this, He also wants you to be fruitful in His relationship with you. Make Him the center of your life. Then watch how He showers you with His fruitful Grace and Presence in your corner of the galaxy. For wherever He goes, the world around Him grows more fruitful.

This is the reason Jesus stated in John 15:5 that you will bear much fruit as long as you remain in Him.

#55 - Do Good

"For this is the will of God, that by doing good you should put to silence the ignorance of foolish people." 1 Peter 2:15

Imagine a world where every person's focus is to seize opportunities to do good for the person next to them!

It comes more natural with those who are close to us, but how about those people not within our inner circle?

Not our next door neighbor, but our next, next door neighbor. Not the person who we have similar interests; but the one whom we have nothing in common.

Want to intentionally be more Christ-like? Why not set a goal of touching at least one other person each day with a little goodness? Ask God to lead you. Watch as a three-fold cord become strengthen. Your relationship with the Triune God. Your relationship with another person. God's relationship with each of you.

Also how about to do good in response to evil thrown your way? This allows you to imitate our Heavenly Father who does the same every day. Besides, it may be kind of fun to watch the perplexed face of others when you respond with goodness. The natural response is to retaliate with a form of violence (Romans 12:20-21).

Every movement begins when one person makes the commitment to act. So why not form a committee of one (you). Go change your corner of the universe by planting seeds of goodness with Christ.

Besides, isn't the Christian life an adventure of sharing God's goodness with each other anyway?

#56 - Do You Trust Your Obedience or Christ?

"He (Jesus) also told this parable to some who trusted in themselves that they were righteous, and treated others with contempt: "Two men went up into the temple to pray, one a Pharisee and the other a tax collector. The Pharisee, standing by himself, prayed thus: 'God, I thank you that I am not like other men, extortioners, unjust, adulterers, or even like this tax collector. I fast twice a week; I give tithes of all that I get.' But the tax collector, standing far off, would not even lift up his eyes to heaven, but beat his breast, saying, 'God, be merciful to me, a sinner!' I tell you; this man went down to his house justified, rather than the other." Luke 18:9-14

Most of the time, we catch our self-judging others based on their outward performance. This is until we come to know their heart.

Jesus in this parable showcases the problem. These two men, a religious Pharisee and an unwelcome tax collector are in the temple to pray. The tax collector is non-welcoming. The people looked upon them as robbing their hard-earned money. On the other side, is the Pharisee. He establishes the cultural, religious standard. Most people at the time believed they were living the way God intended.

As the parable highlights, the Pharisee prayed lifting himself up before God. Meanwhile the tax collector humbled himself. The Pharisee focused his opinion on himself before God. He reiterated all the activity he does. He stresses his obedience to the law and compares his actions against others. In his eyes he is better than the others. Better because he doesn't do sinful acts. Better because he performs religious activities expected of him. He emphasizes his obedience to prove himself more righteous than others.

But the tax collector doesn't look at himself and his actions. Instead he focuses outward toward God. He places the emphasis on His mercy and not his personal actions. Jesus concluded the tax collector' actions were better off than the Pharisee's self-promotion.

Bottom-line: It's about Jesus Christ and not what we do. He clothes us with His righteousness and His actions justify us. We simple do what is expected of us as children of the living God. We don't emphasize our obedience, our faith, nor our acts of service. Instead we place the entire focus on Jesus Christ who makes everything possible. He is our Priest, Savior, and Rabbi. We are his apprentice. He is the master; we are the student. His life, death, resurrection, and ascension into heaven has made this all possible.

We don't emphasize our obedience. Instead we highlight and showcase Jesus Christ.

#57 - Thankfulness is Repentance in Action

"...give thanks in all circumstances; for this is the will of God in Christ Jesus for you." 1 Thessalonians 5:18

Do you? Do you give thanks in every situation? When times are good, like winning the Super Bowl, it sure is easy. But what about those times when the ugly comes knocking at your door? Even worse, when the world around you is dumping their negative junk upon you? When you begin to question your identity in Christ, your strengths, and your worth to serve others? Do you still give thanks?

Being thankful is simply acknowledging He is in charge and not you. It takes the burden from your shoulders. Being thankful reinforces your gratitude for what the Triune God has done, is doing, and will yet do. You come to greatly appreciate His work in your life. Your thanks refocuses your mind and soul toward your Savior and Lord. It helps keep all things in perspective.

Repentance is about returning your focus toward God. When you repent you acknowledge your need for a Savior. When you repent your aim is to reach out for the goodness of God. Your repentance turns your mind away from self and toward your blessed hope in Jesus Christ.

Thus when you extend gratitude and thankfulness, you are putting repentance into action. When you read the Biblical psalms written by King David, you see how he acknowledges his sins. And always ends with thankfulness in his Lord. We do likewise. Always be thankful.

#58 - I Will Be With You Always

"...And behold, I am with you always, to the end of the age." Matt. 28:20

We have a promise from our Lord. He will always be with you. It doesn't matter whether you feel or sense his presence. It doesn't depend whether you did your good deeds for the day or not. It doesn't even matter whether you believe it or not; He is with you.

When your trust in Him reaches permanent belief, you find yourself unwavering. You are at peace no matter the circumstances. You realize your faith is in Him and not how you feel for the day. You accept His Word meant for you. You know what you know because of Him.

When you pray, you reach-out toward Him. His Words come alive in you. His Spirit merges with your spirit to become one. Your attitude and love reflects His. He becomes not only your King and Lord, but a trusted friend; a royal influence in your life.

His love for you is so much greater than we will ever phantom in this life. He loves to abide with you. In Moses time, He had a tent built where he resided and visited with Moses. Today He lives within His Church - His Body - You and I.

It's not magic. It's not your imagination gone wild. It has nothing to do how you were raised within your family. It is all about Him. When He promises, He delivers. May not be according to your schedule, but always on time. Not your time, but His. As we have learned, our Lord seems too always arrive late according to my schedule. But the fact is He arrives because He hasn't gone anywhere. He is always with you.

#59 - Just Because You Can Doesn't Mean You Should

"All things are lawful for me, but not all things are helpful. All things are lawful for me, but I will not be dominated by anything." 1 Corinthians 6:12

While driving your car in most states in America, you are allowed to make a right hand turn on a red light after your stop. It doesn't mean you have too, but you can.

In America, you can also apply for whatever job you want. You may not have the skills and temperament, but you can. Again, it doesn't mean you should, or qualified, but you can apply.

Likewise in America, you have the right of free speech. The law allows you to express yourself with the protection of the government. Again, you have the right to say what you want but it doesn't mean you ought too.

Just because you can do something doesn't mean you should. At the intersection, if someone is crossing the street your turning would be a major accident. Just because you can apply for a job, you are short-changing everyone if you aren't qualified for the work. Again because you don't agree with someone doesn't mean you abuse their character.

Because you can doesn't mean you should. Chocolate is a favorite food for many. But there are those like myself that can't control the amount we eat. Thus, rather than be a slave to its gluttony desire, we find it best to stay away. Sex is a strong desire with much pleasure. Yet outside of marriage, it becomes a physical addiction. You can also have as many gods as you desire. But if the Triune God is not first and central, you are wasting your energy on worthless idols.

The bottom-line: You can if you so choose, but are the consequences worth it?

#60 - Non-Fatal Failure

"For I, the Lord your God, hold your right hand; it is I who say to you, 'Fear not, I am the one who helps you.'" Isaiah 41:13

In business over the years, we have seen how fear of failure has dismantled the career path of many leaders. If you haven't come to that point yet where the decision you need to make is so overwhelming, then wait. You haven't yet faced your worst enemy.

Whether the decision is to sell your business to a competitor. Or fire a key employee. Or take on more debt for the sake of unknown growth. Many executives and managers have struggled and anguished through the process.

Yet I am also amazed how certain entrepreneurs fearlessly face the same dilemma. They step back, view the unknown horizon, and make a prudent decision. The main difference is the refreshing faith of the entrepreneur. Their attitude shouts out that whatever happens is non-fatal in the long term.

Yes, one may economically dissipate everything that took years to acquire and build. And yes when one associates success with self-worth, the burden can be overwhelming. Yet let the truth be told. These men and women have learned that the outcome will not diminish one's value as a person. In other words, failure is non-fatal.

As a Christ-follower, we have learned one's relationship with the living God is the most important thing. Everything else is secondary. The outcome of what lies ahead doesn't matter in the long term. One can walk away from everything and know that with God's help everything can be restored.

The difficult challenge is not the acquisition of the physical toys. But the fortitude of character built from inside your soul. This is what God desires you express through the world around you.

The pain for most believers is "not the what is in it for me battle." Instead it is the concern for the weaker minds and hands of those who are dependent on you for their livelihood. Most people who surround you are probably more focused on what you can give them. Rather than trust the living God to provide everything for all.

Failure most often is the starting point toward learning who God is and how you can join Him in His work for mankind. Failure is painful when you place your trust in the outcome to solve all your problems. Failure is also a problem when you accept your god as the solution rather than the obstacle to overcome. But with the Triune God, failure is never fatal. Only the starting point of discovering who you are in Christ.

#61 - Time & Chance

"Again I saw that under the sun the race is not to the swift, nor the battle to the strong, nor bread to the wise, nor riches to the intelligent, nor favor to those with knowledge, but time and chance happen to them all."

Sorry to disappoint you if you haven't yet discovered the fact that you are not in total control of your life. Yes you can control your response to life, but you cannot always control the outcome. Many have tried and not one has succeeded from beginning to end.

You did not choose the time and place nor parents of your birth. You most likely will not choose how and when you will exit this world. You may think suicide is your ability to control the outcome of when and where. But again not all who attempt succeed. Other people do have a say of what you do.

Professional sports is a good example. We look at the stats and determine who is the better team. Yet great teams have bad days and mediocre teams over-achieve. This is why we play the game. Everyday life is the same.

You may have a plan for life, but is everyone on board with it? Will the government cooperate and make it easy for you? Will the piano thrown out of the 10th floor skyscraper window unbeknownst to you find its mark on top of your head? Will lightning strike and burn your dry backyard preserve before being extinguished? Will the speeding car driven by an unknown drunk driver fail to stop at the intersection? Even though you are an excellent defensive driver, he collides into you from your blind spot.

Things happen in life that are unpredictable. You and I cannot control every event. Your odds of being struck by lightning are better than the odds of winning the Power Ball lottery. Yet will either ever occur in your lifetime? Yes it could happen. But is it something you can plan and control to happen?

The earlier you learn what you can and cannot control will make your life more enjoyable in the process. Yes you need to plan but also have alternative routes when events don't work out as you anticipated. Yes you need to control your response to a situation. That is what maturity is all about. And yes you can choose which relationships you will nourish. Also which ones you will extend more grace toward.

But more importantly, you could choose to follow the Rabbi's Rabbi - Jesus Christ. He wants to share his life with you as you share yourself with him. It definitely makes the journey more adventurous. More enjoyable. More favorable. All while you deal with the circumstances and events life throws your way.

#62 – One Another

"Therefore, accept one another, just as Christ also accepted us to the glory of God." Romans 15:7

Sometimes when I hear a phrase over and over, I like to search out the Scriptures for clarity and purpose. This past week the phrase "One Another" jumped out at me during a weekly sermon. It had nothing to do with the main message. He expressed this one short phrase in the middle of a story. So rather than write on the subject, I copied the verses for you to read yourself. They are self-explanatory. They showcase how God's children experience life in community.

"For this is the message which you have heard from the beginning, that we should love one another." 1 John 3:11

"...no one has seen God at any time; if we love one another, God abides in us, and His love is perfected in us." 1 John 4:12

"Be hospitable to one another without complaint." 1 Peter 4:9

"As each one has received a special gift, employ it in serving one another as good stewards of the manifold grace of God." 1 Peter 4:10

"You younger men, likewise, be subject to your elders; and all of you, clothe yourselves with humility toward one another, for God is opposed to the proud, but gives grace to the humble." 1 Peter 5:5

"Therefore, confess your sins to one another, and pray for one another so that you may be healed." James 5:16

"Do not complain, brethren, against one another, so that you yourselves may not be judged; behold, the Judge is standing right at the door." James 5:9

"But encourage one another day after day, as long as it is still called 'today,' so that none of you will be hardened by the deceitfulness of sin." Hebrews 3:13

"...and let us consider how to stimulate one another to love and good deeds," Hebrews 10:24

"Therefore, encourage one another and build up one another, just as you also are doing." 1 Thessalonians 5:11

"Live in peace with one another." 1 Thessalonians 5:13

"...and may the Lord cause you to increase and abound in love for one another, and for all people, just as we also do for you;" 1 Thessalonians 3:12

"Now as to the love of the brethren, you have no need for anyone to write to you, for you yourselves are taught by God to love one another;" 1 Thessalonians 4:9

"See that no one repays another with evil for evil, but always seek after that which is good for one another and for all people." 1 Thessalonians 5:15

"Do not lie to one another, since you laid aside the old self with its evil practices," Colossians 3:9

"...bearing with one another, and forgiving each other, whoever has a complaint against anyone; just as the Lord forgave you, so also should you." Colossians 3:13

"Let the word of Christ richly dwell within you, with all wisdom teaching and admonishing one another with psalms and hymns and spiritual songs, singing with thankfulness in your hearts to God." Colossians 3:16

"Do nothing from selfishness or empty conceit, but with humility of mind regard one another as more important than yourselves;" Philippians 2:3

"...with all humility and gentleness, with patience, showing tolerance for one another in love," Ephesians 4:2

"Be kind to one another, tender-hearted, forgiving each other, just as God in Christ also has forgiven you." Ephesians 4:32

"...and be subject to one another in the fear of Christ." Ephesians 5:21

"For you were called to freedom, brethren; only do not turn your freedom into an opportunity for the flesh, but through love serve one another." Galatians 5:13

"But if you bite and devour one another, take care that you are not consumed by one another." Galatians 5:15

"Bear one another's burdens, and thereby fulfill the law of Christ." Galatians 6:2

"Be devoted to one another in brotherly love; give preference to one another in honor;" Romans 12:10

"Be of the same mind toward one another; do not be haughty in mind, but associate with the lowly. Do not be wise in your own estimation." Romans 12:16

"Owe nothing to anyone except to love one another; for he who loves his neighbor has fulfilled the law." Romans 13:8

"Therefore, let us not judge one another anymore, but rather determine this – not to put an obstacle or a stumbling block in a brother's way." Romans 14:13

"So, then we pursue the things which make for peace and the building up of one another." Romans 14:19

"If I then, the Lord and the Teacher, washed your feet, you also ought to wash one another's feet." John 13:14

"By this all men will know that you are My disciples, if you have love for one another." John 13:35

#63 - The Benefit of Capitalism

"Thus says the Lord, your Redeemer, the Holy One of Israel: "I am the Lord your God, who teaches you to profit, who leads you in the way you should go." Isaiah 48:17

Capitalism is simply an economic system. The system allows people to own property and trade with others without interference. The decision whether to buy or sell is between both parties. Each party owns something and exchanges the item at a price mutually acceptable by the other. There are no outside influences who have final say of the matter.

Today's garage sale is a good example of a capitalistic system in action. The homeowner owns used clothes, toys, and tools that they no longer need. Yet, the items may still be valuable to someone else. So, they advertise in the weekly paper and hold a one day sales event selling their wares at the best price. Often, people negotiate a price acceptable for both sides.

Pure capitalism is rare. Most places where capitalism thrives, the government creates laws to allow it. The moral fiber of the people police it. The freedom it allows creates an environment for opportunity to be rewarded. But also the naive and innocent to be harmed. The fruit of capitalism is generally a byproduct of the heart of its people.

With capitalism, the individual owns the property and not the government. The property includes real estate and ideas. The owner has the right to convert her property into monetary means. This is done as an exchange for services, products, or cash by another person. The exchange is a mutual agreed price.

Those who oppose capitalism most often blame the system rather than the person. They ignore the heart and moral fiber of a person. The same issue arises with violence and guns. Instead of focusing on the heart of the person, the blind solution is eliminating the tool. The same in regards to overdoses and drugs. The same can be said for a host of other harmful acts conducted by people against themselves or others.

In a free economy astute people understand that labor leads to savings. Savings builds capital. Capital allows investment into businesses and ideas. Businesses and ideas produce wealth.

Everyone in a free economy has the opportunity to work, save, and invest for a wealthy lifestyle. But, many choose to bypass the savings/investment route. Instead they jump into debt so they may experience the "good life" now. The result is slavery to a lender, one's possessions, and a bleak future.

What needs to change for a people to flourish is a matter of the heart. This is a subject politicians avoid. Greedy business people exploit. Religious hypocrites deny the real solution. When the hard heart of a person melts in the hands of their Creator, capitalism is the ideal. It becomes the ideal human method to bring about human flourishing for all parties. This includes the rich, poor, male, female, educated and uneducated. When capitalism is built upon the foundation of God's Grace and Truth, people flourish. Individuals grow. Families are provided for. The community experiences the richness of our Creator's wealth. A capitalistic system makes it easier for you and your neighbor to enjoy more of the fruits of their labor.

So don't blame capitalism for our problems. If you think a better system would be socialism or another ism, think again. When you view history and facts, socialism has never worked and led to the destruction of many. Capitalism though has taken more people out of poverty than any other system.

But more so, focus on the Source who made every good and profitable system in the universe today. Connect with Him and allow your roots to be fed and nourished through Him. Capitalism or no capitalism, you will come to experience the richness and Shalom of life within Him and through Him.

#64 – What Is the Good Life?

"The thief comes only to steal and kill and destroy; I came that they may have life, and have it abundantly." John 10:10

How would you define the good life?

Married to the perfect spouse? Children who behave like angels at home and away? Neighbors who care for you and your success? Work that is fulfilling and rewarding? Material comforts where you have no needs? Physical health abounding with energy? Time to experience the beauty of creation and the fruit of your work? And (add whatever else you believe it will take) to fulfill the good life?

Does your life look like this? Or is it almost the opposite? Yet Jesus came so we could have a life overflowing with abundance. Where is mine you may ask?

There are those who equate ones faith with wealth and health. If you aren't healthy or wealthy, you must be lacking in faith. (This is their erroneous self-righteous belief). Others are satisfied if only one area of their life meets their expectation. Yet Jesus came so we could have a life overflowing with plenty. Isn't this what he is quoted as saying? Did he forget you and me?

The good life isn't measured in quantity. Nor is it measured by external luxuries. Instead, the good life is the outer expression of an inner treasure. When we surrender to God's Will, we allow Him to live in us. The outcome is His goodness being expressed through you and I.

None of us are good; only God (Mark 10:18). When His character is allowed to be exemplified through you and me, goodness shines. The longer we allow His goodness to shine through us, the more impact His goodness has in the world around us.

The good life is allowing the Triune God to manifest Himself in you and through you. The beneficiary is you and those you come into contact with each day. The more you hang out with Him, the more His goodness rubs off on you and others. You will only frustrate yourself without His Spirit merging with your spirit. With God's presence living in you comes the full measure of His Spirit. This includes love, joy, peace, patience, kindness, goodness, faithfulness, gentleness, and self-control.

Want the good life? Build a yielding, personal relationship with Jesus Christ. Allow His Spirit to lead you. As you do, you will experience the good life. And yes, the inner life leads to a pretty good outer life. But the outer life is simply the eternal expression of a good inner one.

#65 – Grace Unlimited

"And after you have suffered a little while, the God of all grace, who has called you to his eternal glory in Christ, will himself restore, confirm, strengthen, and establish you." 1 Peter 5:10

What is grace?

Many people I speak with seem to think it has only to do with the forgiveness of your sins. Others believe it is so much more. I being one.

Grace is simply defined as "unmerited favor." Yes our Lord Jesus extended His grace upon us by removing mankind's Sin of rebellion. But grace is so much more.

When Peter preached his first sermon on the Feast of Pentecost, he quoted from the prophet Joel. Joel prophesied that in the latter days God's Spirit will be poured out upon all humanity. The result is a manifestation of acts leading toward human flourishing. God extended His grace upon us through His Spirit. The result is humanity's explosion of experiencing the richness of this planet. God is in the business of distributing His grace upon us because He is the source of everything good.

It does not matter whether we pursue Him or not. His goodness and unmerited favor is showered everyday upon this planet. He feeds the ignorant and unjust. He hears the prayers of every person no matter their denomination or belief. Whether He answers or how He answers is another matter. But He knows. He grants unmerited favor upon people who serve His purpose. He allows the unrighteous to live longer than others. He knows it may take time to breakdown their hard hearts.

When suffering seems overwhelming, He showers us with His grace. When the solutions are few, He pours His unmerited favor upon us. Yes we may hurt for a moment, but He is there to help carry us through. He is the author of grace and the sustainer of grace. He realizes our fragility. From His love, we experience His favor not because who or what we do, but because of who He IS. We don't earn or buy His favor. Instead we place our trust in Him and allow His natural self to rub off unto us. We realize the more we come to know Him, the greater is our appreciation. The deeper we develop an intimate relationship with Him, no problem seems insurmountable. We are confident that in due time everything else will work out because of Who He IS.

Grace unlimited. How sweet the sound.

#66 - What is Your GQ?

"Be still, and know that I am God. I will be exalted among the nations; I will be exalted in the earth!" Psalms 46:10

We all have heard about Intelligence Quotient (I.Q.). And most of us are probably aware of Emotional Quotient (E.Q.). But how many of us focus on improving our G.Q? Our Godly Quotient.

We spend our lifetime accumulating knowledge. Yet most of what we acquired is only good for trivia game shows. As we mature and gain control over our emotions, we discover something new. We find our success has more to do with our attitude than our intelligence. That our actions rather than our words are more important. That our focus on personal goals/dreams keep us occupied. Thus we forgo the expectations and standards of the outside media/culture.

Your Intelligence and Emotional Quotient may add insight into your strengths and abilities. But it is a far cry from the most important measurement: your relationship and knowing the Triune God. When you become more aware of God's presence in your life, your faith grows. Knowing He shares His name with you, your assurance in Him grows. Encourage by His desire for you to succeed in life, you find yourself in a wonderful awe state of mind, heart, and soul. As you lean more on Him, He opens more of your eyes and ears to see the work of His hands in your life and in others.

You ask in prayer and observe the answers. You seek to add value, and find. You knock on doors until the one opens that takes your breath away in amazement. You come to realize each day there is a God and He is involved in every detail of your life. You become more and more comfortable in trusting

Him through the hard times as well in the good times. You come to better know His ways. Yet you are always surprised how He works-out situations. The circumstances are beyond your initial expectations. Your God quotient grows every day.

Intelligence is good. So is strengthening your emotional management skills. But nothing compares with excelling in your awareness of God Himself. To favorably experience His love and influence in your life is tops. Make that your aim and everything else seems to fall into place better than you could ever realize.

#67 - The Relevancy of Jesus Christ

"but these are written so that you may believe that Jesus is the Christ, the Son of God, and that by believing you may have life in his name." John 20:31

A little more than two thousand years ago, a baby was born that would change human history. He grew up and started a movement. He did so without writing a book. He didn't run for political office. He didn't lead an army. Nor did he corner the economic markets. He was born into an unpopular ethnic group. He surrounded himself with people from all strata of society. He was very controversial with his working peers. Yet today this man is the central figure of an international religion. A religion that integrates all nationalities, sexes, races, social, and political groups.

He still appears on magazine covers. Books are still being written about him. His story continues to be translated into multiple languages. His impact into the lives of people living today is an ongoing witness for unbelievers. Eventually you either acknowledge him or deny him in your life. You can only ignore him for so long.

For if HE is the Son of God. If HE is the second person of the Trinity. If He is King of Kings and Lords of Lords of heaven and earth. If He is the Savior of all humanity. What does that mean for you and me? How would knowing that change your life? Your purpose? Your future? Your family? Your relationships? Your work?

You see atheists try to prove Him an imposter. Then reach the conclusion He is who He claims to be. You read books by the saints of yesterday and today. Then you yourself experience the impact of walking in the Spirit. You can only receive assurances that there is more to this Man-God that even the Bible explains.

When you remove the commercialism. When you put away the pageantry of holy days. When you strip away the false illusions of people. Then you come to realize with gratitude the graceful act of HIS benevolence. All from a God who cares so much to become one of us. For if humanity was worth nothing more but the value of a rat or a dog or a horse, would they be worth redeeming?

HE became one of us so we can become one of His.

#68 - Real Love And Real Truth

"Little children, let us not love in word or talk but in deed and in truth." 1 John 3:18

Love without Truth is not real love; and Truth without Love is not real truth. For Love and Truth is based on Reality. And Reality without God is a fantasy. For God is the author of Love and Truth.

Love and Truth are not a human creation. Humanity discovers Love and Truth in the world around them and through people. For Love and Truth are the backbone of God's character. His divine nature exemplifies Love and Truth throughout His creation. When Reality is confirmed, truth is revealed.

Truth is not the perception of an individual. Nor the feelings of a group of people, but the repeated outcome of history. Likewise Love is not just an act or feeling. But the servitude attitude of heart toward another person. The focus is on their success and well-being turned into action.

When one comes to know God, then one also comes to know real Love and Truth. Truth with a capital "T" is a person known today as Jesus Christ. Truth with a small 't" are the divine values and principles built upon the Triune God's character. HIS truth is on display throughout the creation of the world.

If one wants to know what real Love and Truth is like, then one needs to do business with the Creator of Love and Truth. As a mutual relationship builds between you and HIM, you will come to know HIM better and better each day. You will then come to better discern between real Love and Real Truth. You will have come to know the author of Love and Truth.

Don't be fooled by artificial love and faddish truth. They are expounded by this world's humanistic systems. Instead study the Word of God as revealed in the Bible and come to know HIM who is Love and Truth.

#69 – Perfect in Christ

"And every priest stands daily at his service, offering repeatedly the same sacrifices, which can never take away sins. But when Christ offered for all time a single sacrifice for sins, he sat down at the right hand of God, waiting from that time until his enemies should be made a footstool for his feet. For by a single offering he has perfected for all time those who are being sanctified." Hebrews 10:11-14

How many prayers must you offer to God so you feel cleanse of your sins? Or how many good acts of service must you perform so you feel worthy to approach the throne of grace? Or how many dollars must you donate to wash away the guilt that clings to your soul?

The answer: just one may be too many.

What Jesus accomplished at the cross was to free you and me. HE freed us from the daily rituals of sacrificing animals (or whatever) as a peace offering to God. Instead HE paid the price as our substitute. His actions made everything right before our heavenly Father. In Christ, we have been cleansed from all sin for ever more.

Yes we will continue to sin in this life. We will commit sins of omission and commission. We will be the target of sin from others. And we may have to pay the physical consequences of sin. But, our eternal home and relationship with our Heavenly Parent is always available. There is nothing we can do to make it better or worst. Jesus himself has made it perfect for us. In Him, we have all the riches and treasures of heaven and earth at our disposal. Not because we are perfect, but because He is perfect and through His perfection we are known.

So enjoy your perfection in Christ!

#70 – Christian Culture is Not the Kingdom of God

"For the kingdom of God is not a matter of eating and drinking but of righteousness and peace and joy in the Holy Spirit." Romans 14:17

The early church saints had a debate about whether it is OK to eat unclean foods. This led the apostle Paul to write in a letter which we now classify as the fourteen chapter in the Book of Romans. The issue revolved around whether it is more spiritual to be a vegetarian or not. Paul's conclusion emphasize the fruit of God's Kingdom is not food and drink. But the attributes of righteousness, peace, and joy.

Most of us probably have never been exposed to God's Kingdom until now. Thus we should hold off judgment until we experience the real thing. The closest we may have come would most likely be a Sunday church service among other Christians. Yet even there God's Kingdom may not be fully operating. Instead we witness a culture where everyone speaks and acts in a Camelot fashion. So where do we go to discover the real McCoy?

The Kingdom of God is HIS reign. God's reign is active wherever people allow Jesus Christ to be the center of their lives. Where HE is served first within all relationships and transactions. Where HE is the final judge on all matters. Where our hearts and minds and souls yield to HIS Word, HIS priorities, and HIS values; not as we determine but as it is.

Reality composes of knowing HIM. When we gain knowledge of HIS ways, we begin to see HIS Spirit at work in our lives. We see HIM active in the lives of others. We begin to experience life the way HE intended to be. As we learn to pray and ask and listen, we begin to see our requests actualized. Dumbfounded but in wonder, we become more and more amazed at HIS ability to bring events into reality.

So where do we find the real McCoy?

Wherever HIS people live, breathe, and serve under the authority of their King Jesus, HE is there. And not only is HE present, but the fruit of the Spirit grows. Like a tree that blooms in the spring time, the impact of HIS Kingdom becomes noticeably alive. It could be in a local church service, or a family gathering, or even in the marketplace at work.

When you see the manifestations of God's Spirit in people's lives, HE is there. When you see people's hearts, minds, and souls yield themselves to their King, HE is there. That is where you will find His Kingdom. Where HE is with HIS people so is HIS Kingdom.

#71 - Your Vocation Is Your Ministry

"As each has received a gift, use it to serve one another, as good stewards of God's varied grace" 1 Peter 4:10

One of the more difficult aspects of Christ-like living is restructuring our thinking. It is said re-learning takes three times more effort than doing so from the beginning. For most of us, we are set in our habits, thought patterns, and perceptions within the first 20% of our lifetime. The remaining years we either spend fine tuning them or redressing them. This is also true for Believers. We are morphing into a new creation. We are being transformed into the image of Jesus Christ. So much so that our new friends and family members would probably not even recognize the old person of yesterday.

One of the areas we begin to change is our perception of ministry. Initially we may see ministry as something the church leadership does. Later we may see ministry as those other people helping the less fortunate. It is only later that we see ministry more wider as simply serving those around us.

Somewhere in time we been educated to believe ministry is something solely spiritual. That every other occupation is secular. Yet the Bible shows us that God sees everything as spiritual AND physical. He doesn't segregate the two. He knows we need both the physical elements to live and breathe and the Spirit to live up to our human potential.

A good example is work.

How does God provide food, clothing, and shelter to people? Does HE not work through people? Especially those who are gifted in their roles within the business community. As they serve one another are they not exercising their gifts in their service for one another?

When the early Church ordained deacons to serve the widows and orphans, who did they select? Did they not select men full of the Spirit of God and gifted for the responsibilities? God has ordained the institutions for the role of providing human care. God provides a place for all to serve one another with the gifts He has graced us with. One can serve within any one of the institutions built to help the human soul flourish. In government, family, or business, each provides the means for a believer to serve. The same is true within all other moral upbuilding industries.

So the next time you feel less worthy in your vocation, remember God has gifted you to serve others. Your role is as important as any pastor or church minister in the eyes of God. Thus ask yourself, how can you best serve others in your marketplace?

#72 - Dull, Blind & Ignorant

"The Holy Spirit was right in saying to your fathers through Isaiah the prophet:
"'Go to this people, and say,
"You will indeed hear but never understand,
and you will indeed see but never perceive."
For this people's heart has grown dull,
and with their ears they can barely hear,
and their eyes they have closed;
lest they should see with their eyes
and hear with their ears
and understand with their heart
and turn, and I would heal them.'" Acts 28:25-27

Do you recall a time when you looked but never actual saw what was happening? Or heard someone speak to you, but never grasp what they were saying? Or even gave a factual answer but never understood the significance?

When the apostle Paul preached the gospel to the Jewish leaders at Rome, his frustration came out. He finished his discourse with the above passage from Isaiah. He called his audience a people with dull hearing, blind eyes, and ignorant of God. Yet he also gave them a way out. If they were willing to acknowledge their inability to hear, see, and comprehend. Then accept his message, they will be healed by God.

The Bible calls this repentance. To make a 180 degree turn from self to God. To turn away from sin and toward holiness. Away from prioritizing your estate as #1, to serving Jesus and His Kingdom as the primary focus of your life.

It is not until an addict can acknowledge their problem, before healing can take place. The same with God. A person needs to accept the reality of their hopelessness apart from God. Until then, spiritual healing cannot take place.

So how about you? Are you having trouble listening, perceiving, and comprehending? If so, maybe it's time to do some serious business with our Lord and Savior. He is a professional at restoring life to His original intention. He can do the same with you.

#73 - Bold Confidence

"...in whom we have boldness and access with confidence through our faith in him." Ephesians 3:12

The Hebrew view of faith from the Old Testament emphasized Chutzpah. Or high confidence. Not a mental exercise. This concept is also re-emphasized in the New Testament from the Book of Hebrews. Faith is more about knowing you know. It is based on the living experiences you walked through. Not some analytical dream you conceive in your mind. We sometimes like to make practical applications into something religious or mystical. But faith is that bold confidence your body, soul, and mind expresses when you are faced with a challenge.

How is this faithful confidence built? Isn't it through life's experiences? When we try something new and learned from the experience, don't we grow our confidence? When we try and fail or succeed at something, don't we gain confidence in the process? Isn't it the same in our relationship with our Lord?

Yes we can have confidence apart from our Lord and in ourselves or abilities. But that isn't the bold confidence we are speaking about here. That confidence is built solely on human skills and abilities. They will eventually fail you. The Chutzpah we are writing about is that bold confidence you develop when you leaned on the Lord. When in hindsight you know HE carried you through the ordeal.

It is eating food and drinking water every day for forty years in the desert. Just like the nation of Israel in their exodus march. It is like a teenager defeating a lion and a bear to defend his family's sheep like David. It is a beauty pageant winner standing before the autocratic King to save her nation. Like Deborah risking her life to save her people. It is a confidence built through the actual experience of trusting God.

It starts with the small things in life and grows from there.

We have been given faith by the Holy Spirit. But unless you use your faith, you will never experience the joy of knowing your heavenly Father. Nor the riches He shares with His children.

Faith is fully alive when confidence exudes boldness. But it only starts when you place your trust in the God of reality.

#74 - Why Be A Student of the Bible?

"..but man lives by every word that comes from the mouth of the Lord." Deuteronomy 8:3

The Bible is a book that reveals the portal of life. Within its pages are the lessons learned by those who have gone before us. As you peruse each chapter, you come to realize human behavior hasn't changed in since Adam & Eve. Our experiences and desires remain the same for thousands of years. Or as one historian stated, there is nothing new under the sun except technology and fashion.

As you read, you will become a student of history, psychology, and human relations. The Book becomes your manual for everyday joy. Throughout its pages, you discover more of God's character, purpose, and story. You discover where real peace and prosperity comes from and how to attain them. You learn to separate real Truth from the lies thrown your way each day. You come to experience and share the power of love from God's heart.

You also learn to recognize the hypocrisy and fears in yourself and others. But more so, you find the faith which leads to the dismantling of these ugly demons in yourself and others.

As you study the lives of people who encountered God, you share in their experience. You come to realize how much you have in common with them. And more so, over time you come to know the Author of Life and your place with Him. You uncover your true identity. You clarify your purpose which will lead to a more meaningful life of adventure and passion.

You may even come to realize the Book was personally written for you. That the God revealed through its pages loves you and wants what is best for you.

That He wants a personal relationship with you. That He is nothing like the stern grandfather you may have heard from others. Instead, He is the loving Dad who provides, protects, and shares life with all his children.

When you come to the place where you recognize there are more Pros than Cons to study the Bible, then do the smart thing. You make the commitment. In hindsight, it will be one of the best decisions you will make in your entire life time. Or it may be one of those regretful choices that you would have liked to have changed. Either way, your choice today will determine your quality of life tomorrow.

#75 – Follow the Rabbi

"But you are not to be called rabbi, for you have one teacher, and you are all brothers." Matt. 23:8

Jesus was a rabbi. A super rabbi. Most rabbis' are knowledgeable of the text but not all rabbis' interpret the text. Jesus was the youngest of the super rabbis' of his time and truly interpreted the Scriptures. At the start of HIS ministry, HE approached Peter and Andrew and said "follow me I will make you fishers of men." So the youngsters drop their nets and left the family business. They joined HIM to pursue the opportunity to become like their rabbi.

In Jesus' time, it is estimated that one of 10,000 men had the gift to memorize the bible in its entirety. Those who didn't have this gift went on to learn the family trade. With Andrew, Peter, James, and John, the family business was fishing. So when Jesus approached them and invited them to follow him, it was an honor. This opportunity wasn't available for those who weren't gifted with super memory.

For when a Jewish lad turned twelve, it was then determined whether they were gifted to be a rabbi. Those gifted would have at least memorized word by word the entire first five books of the old testament. If one wasn't able to recite the entire text, they were led to follow their father's trade.

So Jesus went recruiting disciples who initially didn't qualify. The apostle Paul wrote later in 1 Corinthians 1:27 "But God chose what is foolish in the world to shame the wise. God chose what is weak in the world to shame the strong." What most of us will eventually come to realize is the outcome depends more on God than us.

When Jesus invited us to the table to become his disciple, he didn't choose you because of your greatness. It wasn't because of your beauty, memory, or skill-set. Instead, HE chose you because HE loves you. HE wants to prove to you and others that it is what God is doing and not what you are doing that counts.

This is Jesus' story. We are included in His narrative. We follow HIM because He is the super rabbi that we want to become like. He is our passion. He is our strength. He is our hope. In the end, it is a humble honor and privilege for us all to follow the Rabbi. How about you?

#76 – Change

"Every good gift and every perfect gift is from above, coming down from the Father of lights, with whom there is no variation or shadow due to change." James 1:17

One constant we all deal with each day is the continual process of change. Change happens every day. In hindsight, one could easily admit that life is designed to produce change. People make decisions that impact your life. Processes change. Circumstances evolve where everything is different today than it was yesterday. When our foundation is shaken, life becomes unstable and unpredictable. The future looks bleak and the current situation unmanageable. Yet there is one constant that always remains the same: GOD.

Malachi 3:6 and Hebrews 13:8 state that HE doesn't change. He is the same yesterday, today, and tomorrow. Jesus summarized his message to his disciples of the blessed life in Matthew 7:24-27. He reminded them you need a solid foundation under your feet when life's problems are thrown your way. The words he spoke before pertained to how we can live a more richer life than we ever imagined. But without a sure foundation, life can be treacherous.

Change with God is a whole lot better than change without Him. When one leans on him through the good times and bad, one becomes reassured that He is always there with you. Instead of suffering anxiety, worry, or self-pity, you realize your trust in HIM. You know something very good is going to come out of the mess you are currently in. Yes you may have to suffer for a while, or longer, but the end will definitely be much better than the beginning.

HE doesn't change. HE delivered the children of Israel. HE leads his Church. HE is also preparing a place for you and me for eternity. We know HE is faithful and committed toward the fulfillment of HIS plan. To birth a new age that will include you and me forever. As He blessed others, He will bless you.

So let's build our life on HIS foundation and watch in amazement what HE will do for you in your corner of the world. Remember, life is like underwear, change is good.

#77 - Does God's Love Abide In You?

"...because God's love has been poured into our hearts through the Holy Spirit who has been given to us." Romans 5:5

When a terrorist commits their act of violence, does God's love abide in them? Would a person who is in love with the Almighty kill innocent people in the name of their religion? As the debate continues, do guns kill people or is it a matter of what is inside the heart of the person?

In John 5:42, Jesus was speaking with the religious leaders who were criticizing him. His comment though was true then and remains so today. "But I know that you do not have the love of God within you." Again in Luke 11:42, "But woe to you Pharisees! For you tithe mint and rue and every herb, and neglect justice and the love of God. These you ought to have done, without neglecting the others."

Without the love of God vibrating in us and through us, we are only empty containers. Hollow puppets seeking fulfillment in all the wrong places. We pursue our goals and dreams thinking we will find the answer there. We cover our hurts and pain through addictions. Some which gives us a momentary escape. But when reality comes back the ugliness of our situation still face us. So like an insane person, we repeat the harmful process over again. At times, the unholy anger may build up until the human spirit explodes in violence.

Instead of allowing the love of God soothe us, we withdraw. We fight to forgive ourselves and allow the love of God to be released. We bind our hostility until our emotional tank explodes. Only when one begins to understand and experience the love of God in their life, nothing changes. Only God provides the victory for wholesomeness and Shalom to become real.

We were born to have a relationship with the Invisible God. The Bible reveals who HE IS. As James 4:8 states, "Draw near to God, and he will draw near to you." He has built within humanity the means for you and I to experience life the way He designed us to function. This is not religion. But a way of life built around having an intimate relationship with your Creator.

So if you have tried everything else and are still running empty, maybe it's time to do business with Jesus. Let Him know you are ready to follow Him. He will lead you. He will live in you via HIS Spirit. In the process, his love will embellish you and you will enjoyably share his love with others. And when someone asks you whether God's love abides in you, you will only smile and place the focus on Jesus Christ. For you know the love of God resides in you. But only because of Jesus.

#78 - Divine Perspective

"For my thoughts are not your thoughts, neither are your ways my ways, declares the Lord. For as the heavens are higher than the earth, so are my ways higher than your ways and my thoughts than your thoughts." Isaiah 55:8-9

I was fortunate to find a mentor who demonstrated what a successful business life was all about. He lived with integrity in his actions and words. Now in the autumn of life, I still appreciate the support and wisdom of those who have gone before me. Why re-create the wheel? Life's lesson have taught me many things. One is how much easier, cheaper, and more effective to build upon the work of others rather than unknown path. The arrow scars from my youth are still there as a reminder that some ways are better than others.

The same with life in general. When one has a choice to follow either the latest guru or the divine designer of the universe, who would you choose? The book by an author who writes one or two best sellers? Or the One who has year after year lead all books as the #1 seller?

Each of us maintains a perspective of the events that unfold before our eyes. For example, three people may view the same accident differently. They are seeing the same situation but from another perspective. The same with us. We may view a situation from a historical perspective rather than a future outcome. The only One who grasps the future is the One who simultaneously views the future, present, and past. He is Lord, Creator, and Sustainer. The Bible reveals who he is. More importantly, He wants you to know He is available to be your mentor. You only have to ask Him. So why not take advantage of such a relationship?

#79 – The Real Thing

"But the fruit of the Spirit is love, joy, peace, forbearance, kindness, goodness, faithfulness, gentleness and self-control. Against such things there is no law. Those who belong to Christ Jesus have crucified the flesh with its passions and desires. Since we live by the Spirit, let us keep in step with the Spirit." Gal 5:22-25.

In my early walk with the Lord, I took upon myself to start a self-improvement program. The purpose was to develop the fruit of the Spirit in my life. Like the eastern religions, I subjected my body through discipline. My focus was to become more godlike. At the time I didn't understand the workings of the Spirit. But only that I wanted to experience the riches of God's Spirit.

Some ten years later, God opened my eyes to His awesome work in me through the Holy Spirit's influence on my heart. In hindsight, the first ten years of being a disciple, I was mistakenly led through humanism to make myself into the image of God. It was through the failed mastery of self-discipline I was introduced to the Fruit of the Holy Spirit. Like I have said elsewhere, I did become slightly more loving, kind, and joyful. But nothing compared to now by allowing the Holy Spirit to have full access into my heart and mind.

Humanism works through habitual discipline to change exterior behavior. This is outside-in work. God though works through His Spirit to change the interior emotional heart. This changed behavior is from inside-out.

When you read the above passage in Galatians, you note that the fruit is not from one's human heart but from the Spirit. When we deny ourselves and submit to the Spirit's influence in our life, the essence of God becomes more alive in us. God's Spirit intermingles with our spirit influencing our soul. The Source is God. The recipient is us and those who we come into contact.

Humanism works from the outside-in. God works from the inside-out.

Humanism is like the imitation wedding ring made from glass. It may look like a diamond, but is made with inferior material. A real diamond cuts through glass; a fake diamond cannot.

Humanism likes to look good from the outside. It acts like the real McCoy, but lacks the internal fortitude. Often, it is all form without any substance.

God's Spirit is the real deal. As we submit to His Will and lean on Him, He resides in us and allows His presence to be made known through us. After you experience the real thing, you will notice the illusions and fakes around you.

If you are tired of working hard to experience God's presence in your life, you may be trying too hard. Maybe it's time to rest in Christ and ask Him to position you to experience the real deal.

You only need to ask Him.

#80 – After the Impact of a Hurricane

"You have multiplied, O Lord my God, your wondrous deeds and your thoughts toward us; none can compare with you! I will proclaim and tell of them, yet they are more than can be told."
Psalms 40:5

God is good all the time. Even when hurricanes hit land.

We sometimes like to think God's business is to protect us from all harm. That we should never experience pain nor discomfort. That every day should be a party without any negative events. Yet hurricanes, tornadoes, earthquakes, volcanoes, and lighting storms come. Don't they reveal our helplessness at the moment? In fact when these overbearing events occur, how do we respond?

Do we blame God for our discomfort? Do we immediately seek ways to control the uncontrollable circumstances? Or do we acknowledge our helplessness before HIM? Do we seek His immediate leadership of the situation?

This is the question for the moment. When some people lose everything and others nothing, is one group holier than the other? Why does good things happen to bad people and bad things to good people? If God is always good, why does natural disasters occur? Why do people have to suffer? Why do some lose their entire belongings and experience the pain of homelessness?

During times like this I have to remind myself God is in charge. Many humans may not believe so. Why? Because God operates with a greater purpose than one person's satisfaction. We see events from our limited perspective rather than God's eternal, universal view. From the same event, we may suffer while another may be blessed. Could it be there is a greater purpose being worked out here that we just haven't grasped yet?

Ever notice how life is designed with natural phenomena built into the equation? Our meteorologists remind us humanity has not yet learned how to control the weather. We can forecast patterns. But we cannot yet manipulate these natural laws in a large scale for our benefit. So the thought of being dependent on a God for our weather is difficult for some people to manage. For a Being to diminish the power of a category five hurricane at will makes one feel very small indeed.

Also God's plan for mankind is not a human utopia in this age. This is only a trial run preparing people today for an eternal home tomorrow. When natural disasters occur, God's love goes into action through the hands and feet of people. They are ones who understand the need to serve the less fortunate with their blessings.

God's Kingdom moves into action through various institutions and services. These domains are designed to lend a helping hand and restore life back to "normality." It is God's goodness being displayed. Otherwise, disasters would lead to a continual downward spiral of destruction. Instead, we see the goodness of God in the restoration of humanity.

I am thankful and relieved that IRMA didn't destroy everything in its path. Yet for those who lost everything, I pray that God leads them and direct their steps to restore all things. For those who were fortunate to escape serious harm, be grateful. But pray we find ways to help our neighbors rebuild their lives. For we are in this all together. We all share life's hardships and challenges. Through this process we gain knowledge and grace of Jesus Christ. For HE is preparing you and I for greater service now and into all eternity.

#81 - Knowing God's Heart Through Suffering

"For I consider that the sufferings of this present time are not worth comparing with the glory that is to be revealed to us." Romans 8:18

Some Christians are drawn to God by obtaining a ticket to heaven. Others come to God by first experiencing the fruit of His hands. Yet most if not all will come to know HIM through the pain in their life.

Suffering is an experience that most of us avoid at all costs. We find ourselves fleeing from those who may be hurting. We don't want to reflect those uncomfortable feelings being with them. Yet the Bible highlights how through suffering we cry out to God. Through suffering we realize our limitations and dependency on others. We come to see a side of life that our human side wants to avoid. Yet through pain, most of us learn to lean on God and actually see Him carry us through our ordeal. It is through the suffering that we come to know the heart of God.

Since He lives in us, we are connected with Him through the Holy Spirit. The Spirit gives us the privilege of calling Him Papa. We are like a blessed child sitting on the lap of their Daddy. While we are being bounced, we are also being entertained. Yet most of us get so busy with life and forget the eternal relationship we have with Him. We need a catalyst to draw us back. Without suffering, most of us would totally ignore God.

So instead of having a self-pity party with the pain you are going through, cry out to your Daddy. Be frank with Him. Be open with Him. Be transparent with Him. He may or may not change your circumstances. But you will discover the internal fortitude (shalom) He provides. So together you both may travel through the pain. In hindsight, you will realize how the hand of God moves you to come to know His heart through your suffering.

God Almighty is your heavenly Dad. He cares for you and wants what is best for you. Like the athlete, short term pain leads to long term gain. Suffering is the least desired route to learn about HIM. But is the most practical way for us to experience the heart of God in our life. So the quicker you can learn to lean on him through the ordeal, the faster you will come to realize HIS hand in your life.

#82 - Kingdom Actions

"We who are strong ought to bear with the failings of the weak and not to please ourselves."
Romans 15:1

This morning while biking I experienced God's Kingdom in action. The bike path takes us through a public park which maintains a 1/2 mile circular track for runners and bikers. No vehicles allowed. But today, a F-150 pickup truck decided to jump onto the track as a short-cut to the football field. As the truck came toward me, it brought back memories of those early childhood bike games. When we played in the parking lot next to the library. It was called "chicken."

Two 8 or 9 year old boys would line up their bikes across from each other on each end of the parking lot. We would count to three and ride toward each other at full speed. The one who chicken-out by turning away at the last minute to avoid a collision would be the loser. The other would be the winner through default. I never avoided the collision as a youth.

As the maintenance truck sped toward me, my youthful "chicken" mentality kicked-in. But, the grown up adult mind quickly came back. I realized a bike collision into a moving truck would cause more damage to me than he. Thus I was ready to get off the cement trail unto the grass knob and give the heavy metal truck the right-of-way. But then the truck turned itself off the trail onto the grassy knob. This allowed me to continue without turning. The stronger gave way for the weaker.

A smile then crossed my face. I just saw God's kingdom in action. Those of us who are stronger, are there to help the weaker. Those of us in position of leadership, are there to serve the team. Those of us who have more, need to serve those with less. When the opportunity presents itself, we are to step aside and help those who are less fortunate. Instead of lording over those who are weaker, we are to serve them.

It may have been a pickup truck and bike, but it was a friendly reminder that God's ways work. How about your world? Where do you see God's kingdom in action?

#83 - Be The Message

"In the same way, let your light shine before others, so that they may see your good works and give glory to your Father who is in heaven." Mattew 5:16

As a rabbi breathes the text, lives the text, and teaches the text, so do their disciples. The most powerful sermons are always unspoken. The best disciple-making method is simply to be the message. Are you living the message?

#84 – Confidence

"Therefore do not throw away your confidence, which has a great reward." Hebrews 10:35

Ever noticed how some people exude confidence no matter the situation? Whereas others fidget, hesitate, and cast doubt without any effort. Confidence is the assurance of knowing who you are. Especially after your strengths and weaknesses are battle tested. But more so, great confidence comes when you know you know God loves you. HE goes before you. HE carries you when times are tough based on continual experience. Real confidence is the balance between knowing yourself and knowing your Maker.

Today many people have a false illusion of how real confidence is developed. Parents raise their children under the illusion of self-esteem. Whether Johnny or Susie fail or succeed, they create the illusion that their child is the best. Johnny may run the race and finish last, but doesn't face the reality of failure. He loses out learning from it. Instead, the parents discard the truth. They believe it is more important for the child to feel good about themselves. They confuse performance with self-worth. They end up damaging the child's natural inclination. They fail to help the child discover their real identity in Christ. They create a platform of measuring their self-worth through performance.

The same is true in our relationship with Jesus. We grow in confidence as we lean on him and witness how he responds to our dilemma. He may not change our circumstances, but will always provide a way for us to move through it. Afterward we will come to know more about ourselves. Also we gain substantially more trust in our Lord.

Confidence is developed when we fail, learn from it, and grow from it. We learn how to succeed and how to properly fail. We learn humility along with confidence. Humility in understanding who we are in Christ and always confident in Him.

No we don't need false adoration, nor flattery to feel good about ourselves. We first need to know who we are in Christ. Then trust him to take us through the ups and downs of life. Through this sanctifying process, we gain confidence and assurance. We come to experience, realize, and know His grip on our life.

#85 - God Prepares a Way

"But, as it is written, What no eye has seen, nor ear heard, nor the heart of man imagined, what God has prepared for those who love him"— 1 Corinthians 2:9

"For we are his workmanship, created in Christ Jesus for good works, which God prepared beforehand, that we should walk in them." Ephesians 2:10

One of the joys of walking with the Lord is knowing He goes before you. Christ-followers have the distinct honor of leaning unto our heavenly Father. They call on HIM to search the best means before them. They do not need to manipulate circumstances or people. Both which causes division and relational conflict.

The fact is God has an eternal investment in you and wants you to succeed in life. But not the way many people think of success. His desire for you and me is to build Christ-like character which leads to a productive life. The problem is most people want a productive life without the character building effort.

God cares for you more than you realize. HE wants what is best for you. HE most likely already has prepared a way for you. Your only challenge is to discover it and walk through it. How does one discover it?

Simple answer: by growing in the grace and knowledge of Jesus Christ. Not only intelligently, but relational. We need to hunger for a love relationship. We need to know Him so well that we can rest our heads on his "bosom and hear his heart beat." We need to develop a relationship with Him were we know how He communicates with us. Is it through His Word? HIS Spirit? Our conscience? That slight nudge? Or that inspired thought that comes outside our mind? How ever HE speaks with us we need a thirst for more of Him and less of us.

Biblically we see how John the Baptist prepared the way for Christ. His Father led Jesus through planned events. All them accumulated to fulfill Scripture and prove He is the Messiah. We see how the Spirit led apostle Paul throughout his ministry. We see the same with many others throughout the Bible. Even Jesus mentioned that he is preparing an eternal place for us.

In summary, you are created to do good work which God prepared beforehand for you to do (Eph.2:10). Lean on Him and He will unwrap it for you.

#86 - Accountability - Maybe

"Therefore let us leave the elementary doctrine of Christ and go on to maturity..." Heb. 6:1

Imagine if God didn't do his job. What if He decided to take time off and leave the universe operating by itself? Without anyone accountable or responsible for its maintenance. Some in fact believe that is precisely what God has done. These are our deists friends. They believe God created the universe. Walked away, and then left everything for us to operate and finish the work. Yet we are reassured throughout Scripture that God is on his throne. HE continues to be involved in the lives of his children. He is not an absentee parent. He takes personal responsibility for the rearing of his children.

Now some of us may prefer to have him neglect his involvement in their life. But I for one appreciates his graceful, untimely interventions. Otherwise this life may have been over a long time ago.

Yet all this leads to a question. "How accountable are we in our relationships and responsibilities?" Do we accept personal responsibility for the development of the relationship? Or do we expect everything to fall into place without effort? Are we accountable too others for the contribution of the relationship? Or expect the other side to do all the giving and we just take? Or are we control freaks who need to dominate and control the relationship?

If we haven't taken the time to understand the impact we have in the lives of others, than now is the time to check. Are we carrying our share of the load or leaving it for others? Maybe it's time to accept personal responsibility for our actions. Are we ready to be held accountable by others? Or is it not time yet to grow up and become the person we were designed to be?

A part of maturity is accepting our role in the lives of others. The list would include our mates, parents, and siblings. Also our neighbors, work associates, fellow citizens, and yes, even God. He's done most of the work already. We only have to accept our role in the matter. Is it too hard of a matter to be held accountable by the King of Kings and Lord of Lords? It's His story. We have the privilege to take part with him and hold up our side of the relationship. And our relationship with Him includes everyone else in our tiny world. So being accountable to others may not be a bad thing. In fact, it may be the one thing still holding us back from experiencing life the way He designed it to be.

#87 - Faith, Freedom, Flourish

"people are slaves to whatever has mastered them." 2 Peter 2:19

Faith leads to freedom and freedom allows people to flourish. The apostle Paul wrote in 2 Corinthians that "wherever the Spirit of the Lord is, there is freedom." He also wrote that "freedom is not to indulge the flesh, but to serve one another humbly in love" (Gal. 5:13).

Ever notice people usually flourish in countries where they are free to live out their faith? When you can choose your future without dominant external influences, you are free. When you have the opportunity to express your God-given gifts with others, you are also free. But countries where people are controlled, the citizens only go through the motions. Behavior is measured without the activation of the inner heart. People may go through the motion without being engaged in the process.

Today many people may think they are free, but their actions define them. Ask yourself, are you the master of your smart phone or the slave of it? Are you free to select what you wear today or subject to the approval of others? Are you in control of your time today or do you allow your watch to dictate your every move?

These are only a sample of questions you can ask yourself to determine how free you really are. No matter your answer, remember we are actually free in Christ. He made it so. You can choose to follow him or not. You can decide to live with Him or apart from him. You can surrender your desires to him or allow your lusts and cravings to rule you. You are free to decide and act upon it.

We all have more freedom than we realize. The question though are we truly living as free people and experiencing its rewards? Or have we blindly enslaved ourselves by living outside the faith of Christ. For remember, Christ-like faith leads to freedom and freedom allows people to flourish.

#88 - Good. Better. Best.

"Do your best to present yourself to God as one approved, a worker who has no need to be ashamed, rightly handling the word of truth." 2 Tim. 2:15

Over the years we have noticed the challenge some people have in making decisions. They typically struggle always looking for the "right" answer. The tenancy usually is the fear of making a "wrong" decision. For some reason, they have never learned the art of making wise choices. If this is you, the below will help you.

For most decisions, the issue isn't right from wrong. For right and wrong are moral dimensions. In most cases, the decision isn't whether something is morally right. But which is the better choice. Now if you were deciding on becoming a prostitute or selling illegal drugs, then we have a moral dilemma. Sin is never a good choice to make. But, for most times the decision isn't whether to sin or not, but to determine which is good, better, or best.

So the next time you are pondering a choice to make, try this. First gather as much information, opinions, and hard facts within your time restraints. Next identify the top three important values you have determined to be. Then review and analyze each option. You will usually end up with one, two, or three options. Pray and ask our Lord for direction. Set a deadline when you have to make the decision. Keep praying, meditating, and evaluating each option before your deadline. Be sure to count the cost in time, money and resources. Are you willing to pay the price with your remaining choices? If not, drop it. When the deadline comes, choose one that your gut is telling you and commit to it.

You will not know which is good, better, or best until somewhere far in the future. So don't fret, question, or become discourage. Instead, exercise your plan. Keep seeking direction from your heavenly Father, and run with it. You may have to make some minor adjustments in the process. But continue in that path until you have hit your preliminary review date. This is a date you established when you made your decision. Its purpose is to determine if the choice was a prudent one. This date you will reevaluate whether to continue moving forward. Have events or circumstances changed? Do you need to quit or readjust you choice?

Generally, you are seeking to make something good. Or taking something already good and making it better. Or turn something better into the best ever. They all are going to be at least good. So enjoy the process, thank God for the opportunity and help, and go make it work. Bottom-line: leave right and wrong for the moral decisions - good, better, and best for all the other choices.

#89 - Building Trust

"Whoever gives thought to the word will discover good, and blessed is he who trusts in the Lord."
Proverbs 16:20

Trust is a two way street. You may want to trust the other person, but can they trust you? Former President Ronald Reagan loved to quote the expression "trust and verify." In my experience with others, this simple advice even works in today's culture.

If you are having a trust issue with another person, you may want to use this approach. Don't trust them with everything at one time. Instead, build trust one promise at a time.

Likewise if you want to be considered a trustful person, behave as one. Don't make promises you can't keep. Instead, when you make a promise, keep it. Live your life with "yes" or "no" as your promise. You will find it takes time for people to trust your words, your character and ability. As they do, your influence for God's Kingdom will be more quickly accepted. Why? Because of your proven actions in the past.

Doesn't God behave the same way with us? When he makes a promise to us, doesn't he keep it? It may not be on our schedule (isn't God always late in our human opinion). But in hindsight we will see how everything works out better than we could ever expect.

An example is Abraham. God put him to the test in potentially sacrificing his own son. He was building a trustful relationship one act at a time. God knew Abraham's heart. Afterward Abraham knew his heart and God's heart. The event led to mutual trust which builds a stronger relationship.

We can do likewise. First become a person who can be trusted. Then work to build trust with others. And always lean on building trust with our Lord in everything you do.

#90 - Let God Change Your World

"And he who was seated on the throne said, 'Behold, I am making all things new.'" Revelations 21:5

Ever great change begins when one person decides to make a difference in the life of another. Every movement begins when one person serves another. Any one act, any one word, and any one thought has the potential to change your world.

Yet potential changes nothing but the fantasy of mere dreams. Real change occurs only when work becomes focus on a specific outcome. When your chosen work aligns with your God-given gifts, value is added into your community. As God champions your mission, you know only time separates your work from completion.

James writes that faith apart from works is dead (James 2:17). That one needs to act out ones belief for faith to turn into positive results. But those beliefs need to be grounded in the reality of Jesus Christ. Otherwise we may be guilty of stealing from Him, plagiarizing him, or even working against him.

Faith also teaches us to rely on Christ for leadership. Instead of seeking God to bless our endeavors, we seek out what God is already doing and ask if we can join Him. Most often, He will joyfully share the spotlight with you. Sometimes though He has other plans and you may have to pass on the adventure. As you rely on your Heavenly Father, you can be assured His Will is already accomplished. You just have to ride the wave toward the shore.

So live each day realizing our Lord may give you something special today. HE may give you one moment, one word, or one act which may positively influence a person's life. Or even the course of human history. Doesn't that make your time and life more meaningful in your relationships? In your pursuits? Think about that...

#91 - Designed To Be Like God

"So God created mankind in his own image, in the image of God he created them; male and female he created them." Gen. 1:27

Imagine a dog behaving like a cat. Or a lion acting like a monkey. Or an elephant like a snake. We would be concern that there was something mentally wrong with the animal. Yet when people behave ungodly, we have come to accept it as normal.

What happens when we fail to pursue holiness, purity, or honesty? Are we not being misdirected from our original design? God created humankind after His image; for God is love, full of joy and abundant in goodness. When we fail to live up to God's design, aren't we losing out on God's best? Satan knows.

Adam and Eve had the opportunity to be more like God. But instead of trusting their Lord, they bit into Satan's temptation. They wanted it all immediately by taking things into their own hands.

Likewise Jesus knew his purpose and design. So did Satan. In the wilderness after Jesus was baptized, the Holy Spirit led him into the desert to face the enemy (Luke 4). Satan made three offers to Jesus. Each was God's destiny for Jesus. But Satan tempted Jesus to immediately accept his destiny. Jesus only had to disobey His Father's Will. We know the event. Jesus resisted the tempter. HE continued to place His trust in His Father to bring about His divine purpose.

We are no different. God has made many promises for us; including to fulfill the purpose for what you are designed to be. But we must patiently wait on Him. We need to resist the temptation to manipulate circumstances for immediate results. Instead to wait on God's timing.

Yes you are uniquely designed. You have a purpose. It may not be what you think it is. But when you lean on our heavenly Triune God, He will direct your steps toward its fulfillment. In the late season of your life, in retrospect, you will recognize God's hand in many of your life's decisions. But meanwhile, while living through them now, you may question, doubt, and worry. Yet as you lean on Him, He will always be at your side reassuring you. HE will coach you. HE is creating His masterpiece in you after His image. So remember, ultimately in this life, it is your purpose to be molded and shaped into the image of Jesus Christ. To be His witness now and in preparation for eternity. Everything else is extra.

#92 - Follow Christ in the Workplace

"So he reasoned in the synagogue with both Jews and God-fearing Greeks, as well as in the marketplace day by day with those who happened to be there." Acts 17:17

Church is in session. No, not just Sunday morning within your faith community, but also 24/7 within your workplace.

Church as described through the pages of the Bible is not a building nor an institution. But people coming together in community. When you come to this realization, it changes everything.

For starters, it unlocks one's mind to the work of God. Typically, HIS saints assemble together to worship, pray, and learn the Word. But is the format followed by your local faith community the only way "to do church?"

As the Bible states, church is people assembled together. People also worship God in various manners. Have you ever questioned the format that is followed? There are common themes mentioned throughout the Bible when saints come together. They may pray, sing, and share the Word with each other (Col.3:16). Jesus himself mentioned that real worship is done in spirit and truth (John 4:24). But my question is can church be done in today's workplace?

What about the small group Bible study that meets once a week around lunch time? Isn't this church in session? What about a private business whose executive team are strong believers? What if they speak, make decisions, and serve their customers from a heart of godliness? Are they not worshipping their heavenly Father by doing his Will on earth as in heaven? What about the prayers being offered for each other during the day? What about listening to worship music with earplugs while preparing a financial spreadsheet? What about the discussions of God's Word taking place at the water fountain? How about the Godly actions of believers being displayed for non-believers to witness each day?

Throughout the work day, are we not witnessing the gospel message to others? Whether through our words, motives, and behavior.

The workplace is our mission field. Where two or more are gathered together in prayer, are they not also being and doing Church? Isn't the Lord among them (Matt. 18:20). It may be unorthodox. It may not fit into a 21st century mold. But when a community of believers gather together, isn't Church in session? When they gather and worship their God with their gifts and talents, isn't HIS Church in session? When Biblical principles, attitudes, and behavior are being displayed, isn't Church in session? When the Word is being preached without being spoken, isn't HIS Church in session?

Don't limit God. Instead let the world see what Church is truly all about. The love of God in community serving others. Worshiping HIM with their individual gifting and talents. Praising Him for His glory. Yes, even in the marketplace.

#93 - Thoughts about Truth

"Then you will know the truth, and the truth will set you free." John 8:32 NIV.

Is truth an opinion or a fact? Is truth subjective or objective? How do we determine what is true? Why is truth important? Or does it really matter?

Your answers reveal the foundation of your life. When you build your house on the basis of truth, you are not gullible to the distorted half-truths of others.

When you have a poor memory, knowing what is truthful and honest allows you to recall the facts. Why? Because you are a person who always acts upon the truthful facts. You don't rely on fantasy, lies, and distortion.

Truth allows you to live a free life without the extra baggage of outside influences. When you know the truth, the truth will set you free. Free from seeking cultural, religion, and social approval.

The closer you are to the truth, the closer you are to the heart of God. The closer you are to the heart of God, the closer you are to the truth. Knowing the truth reveals the heart of God. The heart of God reveals the truth.

Knowing the truth frees you from the false lies and illusions created in our minds. These lies so often causes anxiety, fear, and guilt.

Truth allows you to build a foundation that is immovable. Truth (with a capital T) is Jesus Christ. Truth (with a small t) are the facts built upon reality.

Truth allows you to walk in reality. The author of reality is its creator: the Triune God. Truth allows you to accept reality. For you know who controls reality. You also know your identity within that reality. Thereby you are free to enjoy life the way God created life to be.

Truth matters because it is built on reality. Truth allows you to deal directly with the problem, challenge, and opportunity. Without truth, you are dealing only with smoke. With truth, you can focus on the fire and make it work for you rather than against you.

Truth is found in Scripture. Truth is found in Jesus Christ. Truth is also found in science and math. Wherever the Creator left his imprint, the reality of truth blooms.

There is no fear with the truth. As the truth allows you to discern which way is the best.

Wherever truth speaks, God hears. Whenever truth is revealed, God sees.

However truth is revealed or discovered, God is there. When one walks with Truth, one walks with Jesus Christ at your side.

Truth deals directly with a matter; lies cover up. So, seek the truth. Build your house of life upon the truth, and you will survive whatever ordeal comes your way (Luke 6:46:49).

#94 - Heart Problem?

"And I will give you a new heart, and a new spirit I will put within you. And I will remove the heart of stone from your flesh and give you a heart of flesh. And I will put my Spirit within you, and cause you to walk in my statutes and be careful to obey my just decrees." Ezekial 36:26-27

The nation of Israel once again ran into personal isolation. They find themselves in God's dog house. They have a bad habit of continual rebellion against Him. Rather than focus on their Lord, they repeatedly chase after local gods. This time the result led them to be captured by their surrounding enemies. Yet God, as usual, took the time to encourage them and foretell what He planned to do with them for His name's sake.

Rules and laws are for those who need them. And most of us need them because we do not have a heart that looks at the big picture for the sake of others. Instead we want what we want and we want it now. Our desire and motive is primarily self-oriented.

For example, Adam and Eve satisfying their desire. Did they take into consideration the whole, future consequence of their actions? Yesterday, my craving for French fries. Did I need them? How often are we apt to please our inner desires without a care for the long term effects?

Ezekiel's Scriptural prophecy was fulfilled on the day of Pentecost after Jesus' ascension. There the Holy Spirit made His public display and recruited over 3,000 people (Acts 2). His manifestation caused a revival which led to the start of the Church. Since then, lives are being changed from the inside-out. The fruit of the Spirit began to be seen in the people who surrendered to the

King of Kings (Gal.5:22-24). The heart of stone was being replaced one person at a time.

Today is no different for those who are Christ-followers. They have surrendered to their King. They likewise now experience life with the Spirit. Sin is no longer attractive. Instead the desire to live, play, and work from a holy seat is the joy of the Lord. No longer do we have a heart problem. Instead we have a new heart that mirrors our God (Gal.4:6). A heart centered in Jesus Christ (Eph.3:17). A pure heart that allows us to see the work of God (Matt. 5:8).

So if you are having heart problems, you have direct access to the #1 surgeon of the universe - our heavenly Father. Ask him for a new one. It's His business. And He is very good at it.

#95 - God Waste's Nothing

"When the disciples saw this, they were indignant. 'Why this waste?' they asked." Matt. 26:8

Jesus was visiting Simon the leper at his house. A woman came to him with an alabaster flask of very expensive ointment. She poured it on his head as he reclined at the table. The disciples saw it and became indignant because they believe it was a waste of money. Yet, Jesus' reply was on the act itself which came from her heart. He took the situation and directed the focus toward the gospel message. He also foretold his coming burial, and her worshipful testimony.

God waste's nothing. You and I may look at a situation and develop an expected outcome that we consider good or bad. But God looks at the heart of the people involved. Then HE turns it into a teachable moment for those who have eyes to see and ears to hear.

Jesus was having dinner at a tax collector's house. HE was surrounded with other undesirables (in the eyes of the Pharisees). These teachers of the Law questioned Jesus' association with people who were sinners. Again Jesus took the moment to share the gospel message.

God waste's nothing. What may look like contempt to us, or a challenging moment, may prove to be the changing point in our lives. Every act. Every circumstance. Every situation, is a moment of time God works to create His masterpiece in each of us. God is always working through the good and the bad for our benefit.

God waste's nothing.

#96 - Faith, Character, Wisdom

"...so that your faith might not rest in the wisdom of men but in the power of God." 1 Cor. 2:5

Most people I've met have more faith then they generally believe. There limitations usually came from the poor general education they received from others. Some were placed in positions that limited their thinking. Others soaked in propaganda distorted their view of life. Others surrounded themselves with people who put the fear of the unknown in their heads. And some went the other extreme believing fantasies and lies while living in denial. In fact, most of these people put more faith driving down a two-lane road. They didn't realize the awesome gift they already have in their possession.

Faith comes from God. He allocates as He desires. A little is all you need. The problem is most of us would rather rely on ourselves, or our associates rather than trust God.

When one's journey takes them into the deep crevices of life, nothing will ever be the same again. When the darkness penetrates the soul, and we survive, we grow from the experience. For most of us, it is in the pits of life when we recognize Jesus as He shares His faith, character, and wisdom with us.

After such an ordeal, we realize what real faith is and the assurance we have from Him. We begin to recognize the Godly character and wisdom we lack and desire to have. After such an experience, we want more of Him.

So we may pursue him through religion. But eventually discover how empty and unfulfilling performance-oriented living becomes. We cram our brains reading and studying philosophies of the great minds who have gone before us. But soon realize they don't have the answers either. We may bury our pain with drink, food, or sex. But the demons remain. Only when we surrender our heart to Jesus, will we experience the real fruit of godliness.

When He enters into our life, we learn to follow his ways. When He carries us through our struggles, we learn to trust Him. When He answers our prayer requests, we pray more. When He instructs us through His Word, we gain wisdom for living. When He shapes and molds our character, we experience the fruit of His masterpiece.

Over time, He shows his love for us by molding us into the character, faith, and wisdom He manifests. Grateful we become because of the workmanship He displays in us and through us. With humility we learn to exercise the fruit of His work. He receives all glory, honor, and respect. We know where we came from and now appreciate where we are in the hands of our Maker. He is the Teacher; we are the student. He is Lord; we are His subject. He is the Source; we are the recipient.

#97 - Blind, Broken, Busted

"Because you say, 'I am rich, and have become wealthy, and have need of nothing,' and you do not know that you are wretched and miserable and poor and blind and naked, I (Jesus) advise you to buy from Me gold refined by fire so that you may become rich, and white garments so that you may clothe yourself, and that the shame of your nakedness will not be revealed; and eye salve to anoint your eyes so that you may see. Those whom I love, I reprove and discipline; therefore be zealous and repent. Behold, I stand at the door and knock; if anyone hears My voice and opens the door, I will come in to him and will dine with him, and he with Me. He who overcomes, I will grant to him to sit down with Me on My throne, as I also overcame and sat down with My Father on His throne." Rev. 3:17-21 NASB.

Pride blinds us all. Pride makes us look at the physical dressing around us instead of the inner heart. Pride convinces us that everything is all right. Yet deep inside, we know something is not right. Instead of dealing with the issue, we ignore our conscience and keep doing the same thing. We hope it will go away.

Yet the knocking continues. Even while your bank account keeps growing. Even when your dreams become reality. Even when your fame spreads throughout the marketplace. But that gnawing feeling will not leave you alone.

What is happening?

Your Father God is calling you. He is happy for your success. But wants you to also experience the real treasures of life. So He keeps calling you. He keeps knocking at your door. He is waiting for you to open the door. He wants to break bread with you. But of more importance, He wants to share His life with you.

He wants you to experience real wealth; the riches from His storehouse. He wants to cloth you with the same holiness he wears. He wants to share his authority and influence with you to positively impact the world for others.

So don't ignore him. Don't push him aside. When your inner ear hears the knock, lean against the door. He is waiting with open arms to meet you. When you two meet, you will experience the greatest high this life has to offer.

Compared to Him, we are all blind, broken, and busted. Yet with Him, we are rich. For HE cleans our inner house. He takes away our pride, shame, and pain and replaces them with his rich treasure chest of humility, love, and joy. He changes your life forever.

#98 - Slavery of Religion

"Since you died with Christ to the elemental spiritual forces of this world, why, as though you still belonged to the world, do you submit to its rules: 'Do not handle! Do not taste! Do not touch!'? These rules, which have to do with things that are all destined to perish with use, are based on merely human commands and teachings. Such regulations indeed have an appearance of wisdom, with their self-imposed worship, their false humility and their harsh treatment of the body, but they lack any value in restraining sensual indulgence." Col. 2:20-23

Religion is man's attempt to appease God. The practice and mindset is built around the premise that you are separate from God. If you want God's favor, you have to do something to manipulate God your way. Contrast to real Christianity, where you are already reconciled to God. Not because of what you do, but what the Triune God has already done.

Real Christianity is an abiding relationship with the living God. A relationship built upon the finish work of Jesus Christ. Whereas religion is man's idea of how one must perform to merit God's blessings.

Throughout history mankind has done harmful acts one-to-another in the name of religion. From sacrificing babies at the altar to performing immoral sexual acts, all in the name of their god. In current times, we may have become more civilized. Yet we still have the tenancy to practice religion. When instead we could be enjoying an intimate relationship with the ONE Creator God.

Religious people love to practice self-indulging acts. They may burn candles. Flog themselves. Sacrifice money. Refrain from marriage. Establish higher-than-God-standards of righteousness. Ordain certain days more holier than others. Deny modern conveniences. Clothe themselves in special outfits. Refrain from eating certain foods. Practice special or secret rituals. Refrain from listening to certain music. Place higher importance on "spiritual" occupations. Vote for specific political parties. The list goes on and on and on.

Religion is when the act becomes more important than the heart of a matter. When the task has greater priority than the relationship. If this is you, be careful. You may be emphasizing religion. Wouldn't you rather be enjoying a relationship with the living Lord?

Many times the mechanics of faith are the same. The difficult part to identify is the heart of relationship with our heavenly Father. Only He knows for sure. So why not ask your Father-Son-Spirit how you can improve your relationship with Him? And yes, for those who value religion, don't worry - God also works through religion. You will also find Him in business. Government. Education. Entertainment. Sports. Medicine. And every other institutional field.

For wherever the Spirit of the Lord is, there is freedom (2 Cor.3:17). Freedom from the do's and don'ts of playing religion. Instead we get to experience the richness of a relationship. A familial bond with the God who made everything for us to enjoy.

#99 - Jesus Christ Chose You

"But now he has reconciled you by Christ's physical body through death to present you holy in his sight, without blemish and free from accusation" Col. 1:22

Before you were ever born, Jesus Christ selected you. Before you even heard the name of Jesus Christ, you were forgiven. Before you even acknowledged HIS existence, you were included in the Triune circle.

The Incarnation teaches us these points. God chose himself before the foundation of the world as the sacrifice. HIS sacrifice open the door for humanity's entrance into the heavenly. Entering the world in human form, He (Jesus) clothed himself with the darkness of the world. All sin, deception, anxiety, pride, shame, and blindness was captured within his humanness. God joined humanity and humanity joined God in this act of divine sacrifice.

The result is Jesus Christ lived and died a vicarious life. He represented you and I as our substitute to defeat Satan. HE restored humanity's relationship with our Heavenly Father. In the process, you have been forgiven because of His sacrificial life and death. He did it for you and I.

Not only forgiven, but gave you meaning and purpose. His resurrection and ascension into heaven paved the way for you and I into HIS new creation. He is the first of a new humanity. The physical and spiritual merged together.

HIS act of justification broke down the veil between God and humanity. All humans are included in the circle of life with the Triune God. But sadly many are still ignorant or in rebellion against him. They haven't accepted the reality of Who He IS and our position with Him. There lies our chose. Whether we want to share life with him or not.

The Bible uses several examples to highlight this point. One is adoption. You, the child, have been adopted by the parent (God). Your decision is not to select the parent for adoption. But whether you will become engaged into the family culture. The adoption has already occurred. You can either rebel against your new parent or accept the reality that you have a new guardian. ONE who cares for you. A new home with permanency.

Another example is marriage. In the first century Biblical culture, the woman did not decide who she was going to marry. The selection process was negotiated by the parent and/or groom. As a newly engaged bride, your choice is whether you will respect and be his wife. Will you learned to love him. As a married couple, you can choose to become fully engaged in a mutually shared relationship or not. The consequences of your decision is yours to make.

Lastly, a disciple didn't choose his rabbi teacher. It was the rabbi who selected the student. Many may wish to learn at the feet of a great teacher, but the final decision wasn't theirs to make.

In all three examples the instigator of the relationship wasn't us, but the other side. Our chose is two-fold. First to accept our position in the relationship. Second, whether we become fully engaged in the relationship. The same is true with Jesus Christ. He has already chosen you. Forgiven you. Included you. But will you accept your divine position and become a fully, committed, engaged child of HIS?

#100 – Too Much

"A greedy man stirs up strife, but the one who trusts in the Lord will be enriched." Proverbs 28:25

I recall our daughter as a child of 2 or 3 years old starting to learn the art of communications. Her Mother and I would smile at times when she wanted second helpings at the dinner table. When asked how much she desired, her reply was "too much." In other words, she wanted more than just more.

Being a child, we smiled at the innocence of youth having an open heart and speaking with frankness. Today, she has learned to adjust her behavior and exercise self-control when it comes to food. Yet even today we sometimes tease her with such memories.

But what of the child who doesn't learn the trap that desiring too much can cause? What becomes of them when they reach adulthood? Today's Scripture points to the problem. A greedy person instigates turmoil among the people in their world. Greed may win you more of whatever you desire, but the price is strained relationships. Now if relationships mean nothing to you, then you have a deeper problem. The love of God may be missing in your life.

The good news is the fruit of the Holy Spirit includes self-control. Self-control is of great value for yourself and for those around you. Self-control places a lid on your greed. Self-control allows you to fill your cup with enough to enjoy and share with others. You don't have to be concern with you and others pulled down into the muddiness of sin. Self-control installs boundaries made for you.

So if "too much" is an issue in your life, ask your Heavenly Father to make more room for His Spirit to live and work within you. You will become surprised how much of His Spirit he is willing to share with you. For HIS desire is for your growth and development into the image of his Son.

In fact, if you are greedy, you probably want more of His Spirit. So He can redeem your greed into another masterpiece of self-control. Then you will have a living testimony of God's workmanship to share with others. Just be ready and willing to pay the short-term cost for the long-term gain.

#101 - Brighten Your Corner of the World

"In the same way, let your light shine before others, that they may see your good deeds and glorify your Father in heaven." Matt.5:16

Life is a dance with the Almighty. As you yield your heart and follow His lead you move around the dance floor of life. You find yourself growing in the grace and knowledge of your Lord and Savior Jesus Christ. Your countenance begins to change. Over time, those previous broken areas of your life are now radiant with a newness and vibrancy for life. You have come to the place where you realize the Triune God actually loves you and lives in you.

He not only lives in you, but he is working to transform you from the inside-out. The more you deny yourself for His name sake, the more His light shines through. The more you submit yourself to His healing touch, the more His light radiates through the pain. You come to realize the only good within any person is what God produces. It is then you begin to experience the full riches of His glory.

God especially loves to share Himself with those who draw close to Him (James 4:8). So as He opens our eyes to serve others, He will provide the means. As He opens our ears to hear, His Spirit leads us how to best reply. As He leads us into opportunities to do good, we follow with assurance.

The light others see is God's presence shining through the broken jars of humanity (2 Corinthians 4:7). We no longer hide God's work in us and through us. We are not even concern whether our right hand knows what our left hand is doing (Matt. 6:3). Instead, we let God's love and grace lead us to do good work for His glory. The outcome is His light shining through for others to see.

When you follow the lead of the Greatest Dancer in your corner of the world, people will notice. And you don't even have to try to be noticed. You just let the light of Jesus shine through you each day.

#102 - Biblical Bias

"There is neither Jew nor Greek, there is neither slave nor free, there is no male and female, for you are all one in Christ Jesus." Gal. 3:28

We all read Scripture from a personal bias. Which leads to the question, "what is yours?" Over the years in different seasons of life, I have read the Bible from various worldviews. Like most students, I started from a 21st Century western civilization culture view. Over time, I learn to read the Word from a Jewish Christian perspective. Others may have started from a feminist or humanistic platform. Than others from a denominational background. Or more prevalent today, from a combination of multiple-denominational and non-denominational teachings. The question for today though is "what is your personal bias?"

It is good to know for two reasons. One, it helps identify different positions your brothers and sisters in the Lord hold. Then it also helps you to stay humble realizing there is a possibility you may be in error. So it keeps you open to learn from others.

Today I lean towards a Jesus Centered, Incarnate Triune God worldview. This is my bias. When I read Scripture, I use this as my filter to clarify those difficult sections. It also opens my eyes to understand Jesus' relationship with His Father and with humanity.

For example, take the Scripture, "Greet one another with a holy kiss (Rom.16:16)." Depending on one's view, a different understanding will arise on what a holy kiss looks like. Some of our Arminian friends explain it as a righteous kiss. This is because they associate holiness with righteousness. Again, our humanistic or feminist sister may view a holy kiss as one with passion. Or maybe one that shows respect toward others. Then again, some of our denominational buddies would say it is a command and should be done today. Others agree but establish other norms such as no kissing between the sexes. Some say it was only custom of Biblical times. In the 21st century western civilization we shake hands or hug to show the same love and respect. This is what the holy kiss is meant to portray.

One's preference is not the issue. One still needs to understand the culture of the period being covered. This allows one to determine the application for today's Believer. Some principles are eternal and others are for specific events and times. The kiss is still the cultural norm in the middle-eastern countries today. There men and women greet one another with a kiss on both cheeks. But in America, we hug or shake hands depending on how well we know the other party. So no matter what your preference, the principle is to extend a Godly greeting to the other.

Since God is holy. With holiness define as a multitude of attributes. Like love, joy, kindness, gentleness, righteousness, and self-control. The holy kiss of the 1st century is still a holy greeting in the 21st century. The attitude and heart of the greeting is the measuring stick. Not the mechanical means employed.

So what does this all mean? Simply know your bias. Recognize the bias of others when you read. And always live out Scripture in everyday life.

#103 - Hooks of Expectation

"In the morning, Lord, you hear my voice; in the morning I lay my requests before you and wait expectantly." Psalm 5:3

One of the best ways to build a strong relationship with our Heavenly Father is through prayer. To take time and listen what He has for you shows the importance you place on the relationship. To empty your heart before him is a life-building event. There is no better way to capture the realization that God cares for you and wants what is best for you.

There is one obstacles though you will need to overcome. That is trapping yourself with your expectations. Many times we will go before our Father and ask for something believing it is the best solution to the problem. But the answer does not come the way we expect. God maneuvers the outcome in a totally different way. Because it is not the way we want it, we may become angry with God and give up on Him. Yet in hindsight, we recognize the outcome was better than we could have ever expected.

These hooks of expectations are both a blessing and a curse. To appreciate the blessing, we need to be open to the final outcome. If we limit God to workout events within our little box, it can easily become a curse. God is vastly larger than any box or solution we come up with. His ways impact a multitude of people and events and purposes. Yet He cares for you and wants you to join Him in His adventures. But you have to be flexible and open.

In Acts three, Peter and John went to the temple to pray. There they met a lame man. The lame man ask them for money. Based on Peter's and John's reply, he expected to receive some compensation. But instead of a monetary blessing, the man experienced complete healing.

The outcome was more than he expected. So when we go to God, don't limit yourself with your expectations. Instead allow Him to share His generous heart with you. Not only will you be surprised, but you will come to know Him who is more than you ever realized.

#104 – Soft Love. Tough Love.

"For everything there is a season, and a time for every matter under heaven." Ecclesiastes 3:1

One day the world will wake up. Everyone will recognize what is the central core attribute of this planet. They will see every nook and cranny is built from a heart of Love. At that time life will be lived out like God's original intent. But until then, we who have already met our maker have the honor and privilege to share his ways with others today.

Love is one of those terms which means different things to different folks. The best example I have learned to respect and weigh is how the Triune God relates and deals with me. He knows when to hold and comfort me. He also knows when to hold and discipline me. I call this soft love and tough love.

The basic heart is the same. He cares for me and knows what is best for me. He knows when to push me and when to rest me. He knows my limits and my potential. He is the Master love mechanic.

Isn't that the way we need to learn to be with others?

When my daughter misbehaved, I didn't have to take a rod to her. Instead, one look from the eye of Dad and she knew she needed to change. But I the rebellious teenager was on the other end of the spectrum. When I did something my Mother disapproved, her look wasn't going to change anything. Instead, she took the frying pan and let me experience the full impact of a good swing.

Aren't we the same way with each other? Some circumstances need soft love; other situations require tough love. Jesus himself extended mercy and compassion (soft love) to many of the common folk around him. Yet when he faced the religious leaders and lawyers of his day, he came at them with stronger language. His emotional cuts went right to their heart (tough love). He knew the people involved and the best method to use.

We need to learn the same.

#105 - Broken Bodies, Pristine Souls

"And do not fear those who kill the body but cannot kill the soul. Rather fear him who can destroy both soul and body in hell." Matt. 10:28

This life goes by quickly.

It seems only like yesterday I graduated from high school, married, and raised a family. Now retired from work, I barely recognize the same man in the mirror.

Hard muscles, trim abs, and smooth skin is now replaced with soft hands, a stout belly, and bruised wrinkles. The aging process reinforces inner beauty over outer dress. The character of the soul replaces the facade of dress. Bodies that at one time were fully functioning are now dragging along. Yet beauty becomes more alive as the soul takes preeminence in life.

We have all witness those who are challenged to do what seems impossible. There are those who have no arms nor legs yet function within society. There are those who are wheel chair bound. Yet move about experiencing everything good that life has to offer. There are those who are blind, yet travel through life seeing more than you and I.

Physical limitations are that - self-imposed strait jackets we place upon ourselves. The real battle begins at the soul level. This is where the emphasis is on our heart, mind, and character. Every long lasting triumph worth pursuing begins here. Today we may call it attitudes, smarts, and inner muscle. The Bible calls these a matter of the heart. And wisdom for the mind. The character developed through life's battles.

The bottom-line: teach your children and grandchildren. Teach them to first focus on developing the soul. Let them discover the hidden nuggets written through the pages of the Bible. Learn to listen and follow the Spirit of God. And develop a Jesus-Centered, Incarnate Triune God worldview. The end result? A soul that will thrive under every aspect of your life.

#106 – Pop Theology

"and you will know the truth, and the truth will set you free." John 8:32

Pop psychology, fantasy football, and social networks have one thing in common. They distort reality. A little knowledge may make one feel invincible for the moment. Professionals know. They cringe when another book is written to provide a simple solution to a complex problem. It only makes their role more challenging.

Take general managers of sports franchises. They laugh when one compares their role with fantasy football fans. A little knowledge of building a winning team and fans think they could build a real sports dynasty. And of course, there are social networks. These make one feel connected with others. Though the person on the other end may not be who they present themselves to be. Yet each industry fulfills a need. Thereby creating a large following enriching its creators.

Christianity in the western world is no different. We have distorted the knowledge of who God is through our pop theology. A well-meaning author slices the Gospel message into a cliff note to emphasize its value. Instead of digging deeper into the subject matter, most of us just accept the musical one note. From there we build our internal heavenly vault. Over time though we become frustrated. Instead of experiencing a full, enriching life with God, we struggle with anxiety. We begin to question whether Christianity works.

Take, for example, the concept of Holiness. Western Theology has built a view of God based on a moral science of law. So when we discuss a Holy God, one needs to clarify descriptions. For western theology generally defines Holiness under legal terms. More specific along the lines of righteousness.

When one takes this legal view of God, our view of God becomes distorted. Instead of a loving Father, God becomes a judge looking to punish people. This one attribute of God then becomes our distorted view of who God is.

But when one comes to know who God IS, one comes to see Father-Son-Spirit as a mutual supporting Being. HE is a relational Being full of love, joy, and peace. A God who is full of grace for others. Yet also a God of justice. A God who is for you, not against you. A God who created the entire universe and included you in His plan to share His life with you. Holiness is no longer defined from a legal aspect. But from a relational sphere within the Triune God. God is Holy. Holiness is the full reflection of the total divine nature of God Himself.

So be careful of pop theology. Seek to understand the foundation of any statement. Understand it is only emphasizing one point of the gospel. Realize it's position within the larger picture. And of course, continue to grow in the grace and knowledge of Jesus Christ. As you do, you will not fall victim to the latest pop fad.

#107 – The Great Dance

"How blessed is God! And what a blessing he is! He's the Father of our Master, Jesus Christ, and takes us to the high places of blessing in him. Long before he laid down earth's foundations, he had us in mind, had settled on us as the focus of his love, to be made whole and holy by his love. Long, long ago he decided to adopt us into his family through Jesus Christ. (What pleasure he took in planning this!) He wanted us to enter into the celebration of his lavish gift-giving by the hand of his beloved Son." Ephesians 1:3-6 Message.

Abundant joy. Overflowing love. Insurmountable peace. Ridiculous generosity. Impeccable goodness. Eternal patience. Heartfelt kindness. Child-like gentleness. Atomic-clad self-control. All these are only a few of the elaborate notes that penetrate our soul as we dance with the Triune God.

Like two people waltzing across the dance floor. Both in rhythm to the music of a large orchestra in the background. This is how our relationship with God manifest itself on those unpredictable days. They make up for those other days. When we find ourselves sitting in the funeral parlor of life. When we are leaning on God's shoulder in tears. Listening to the dirge of pain and hoping that this day will quickly past. We long to recapture the richness of His Dance. Both days have their place in life. But of the two, we would much rather spend time on life's dance floor in the arms of the Man-God, Jesus Christ.

Remember those pleasant times when we witness the beauty of our Creator's work. Like the setting sun over the gulf coast on a warm sunny beach day. Or the breath-taking majesty of the Grand Canyon. When we study quantum theory or simple geometry, don't we recognize a mind greater than ours? To witness the birth of a baby leaves one speechless. Or the loving devotion of a mother with her children makes one realize life is so much more than work, eat, and sleep. When one comes to know Father-Son-Spirit and begins to move in step with Him, the dance comes alive. The music, rhythm, and movement of life are enriched with the presence of the Almighty.

We learn to dance with the Triune God through life's challenges and opportunities. We discover there is a time to dance the waltz, cha-cha, and polka. Other times we do the jitterbug, rock-and-roll, or disco. Sometimes we only hold on to each other and sway to a two-step capturing the moment.

When we observe others, they are either moving to the rhythm of life's great dance partner or lost. Sometimes it is like a young daughter with her father at a pre-teen Valentine dance. The movements may be awkward at first but the moment is captured for eternity. The same is true in our relationship with the Eternal.

He wants to dance with each of us. To show us how much more life can be. To reveal what this world has blinded us too. He has already given us a home with an awesome dance floor. We just have to accept the fact that He is the One and be willing to follow His lead through the Great Dance. Remember, as one person told me somewhere in the past, life isn't about waiting for the storms to pass. It's about learning to dance in the rain with Jesus.

#108 – You Belong

"By this we shall know that we are of the truth and reassure our heart before him; for whenever our heart condemns us, God is greater than our heart, and he knows everything. Beloved, if our heart does not condemn us, we have confidence before God; and whatever we ask we receive from him, because we keep his commandments and do what pleases him. And this is his commandment, that we believe in the name of his Son Jesus Christ and love one another, just as he has commanded us. Whoever keeps his commandments abides in God, and God in him. And by this we know that he abides in us, by the Spirit whom he has given us." 1 John 3:19-24

"even the Spirit of truth, whom the world cannot receive, because it neither sees him nor knows him. You know him, for he dwells with you and will be in you." John 14:17

People need people. Humans were made for companionship. We are wired to be connected with each other. We seek to belong. In fact, we shouldn't be surprised. Why? Because the Creator of mankind, the Triune God is likewise a relational Being.

Yet instead of first realizing we belong to God; we seek others to meet all our inner desires. We have a tenancy to seek immediate gratification. So we have our emotional cup filled by various social means. Instead of accepting our identity in Christ, we search for ourself in organizations. We play games with our souls in the workplace, gym, school, bar, church, or non-profit missions. We know God is out there someplace, but admitted He is not the central core of our relationship. What this means is we are missing out in life's greatest dance.

We may not be aware of God's presence. We may be blinded by our faithless glasses. Yet Scripture reveals the truth of the matter. When God is active within you, you know. You know because your behavior aims to please him. You find yourself in love with Him and others to the point you want to help them succeed in life. Your conscience is clean without any regrets as you serve Him. You realize the Spirit of God is producing fruit in your life. You find yourself magnifying your God through your actions and words. You know you belong with Him because His assurance lives within you.

When you are wrong He convicts you, not condemns you. His hand on you is like a loving Father who wants what is best for you. You find yourself changing from the inside-out through a process of His Spirit. Because of HIS fruit in your life, you know you are in Christ and included with Him in the great dance of life. You know who you belong too. You know who you are. You know whose Spirit lives in you. You know you belong. Yes, no one needs to tell you, you simply know - YOU BELONG!

#109 - Jesus Christ is the Good News!

"Then Philip opened his mouth, and beginning with this Scripture he told him the good news about Jesus." Acts 8:35

The Good News is about the person Jesus Christ and His relationship with Father God. Plus the inclusion of humanity within the Triune God circle.

In the last century, the gospel message has quietly shifted away from the person of Jesus. Today the focus is more toward the events of His life. We hardly emphasize his personhood, his incarnation, and his connection with Almighty God. Instead the message most often we hear today reflects the events of his life. Specifically the emphasis is on his death and resurrection. Both acts are significant. But both events are important only because of who HE IS.

Again, the last several hundred years, the gospel message has shifted. We have moved away from the Triune God (Trinity) toward a moralistic Holy God. Today when asked to describe God, many people would first state He is a Holy Being. The Holiness concept though emphasizes a God of righteousness. Whereas the Trinity highlights a God of relationship.

Also today's main stream view of God has more to do with rules and regulations. There is less emphasis on HIS unconditional love, unlimited joy, and overflowing peace. Characteristics HE shares with us through HIS Spirit. Again, many people still view God as a stern, faraway grandfather figure. Not a heavenly Father desiring an abiding, familial relationship with His adopted children.

Likewise, the good news of the Incarnation has been displaced by the passion of the Cross. Today's preachers like to highlight the god of sin and the accomplishment of the cross. How often have you heard a message on the inclusion of the incarnation? That humanity is now included with the incarnate Jesus Christ. Again, the personhood of Jesus seems to take a second position even at the cross.

As stated, the Good News is more about the person Jesus Christ than an event in his life. For instance, if the Good News was only about his death, why did he wait thirty some years before dying. Couldn't he have died earlier as a two year old babe under Herod's killing of children in Bethlehem? Again, the Good News is more than His resurrection. Yes, like all the events in his personhood, they fulfilled Scripture. They accomplished His eternal plan for humanity. But, if He wasn't God become human, all He achieved would be worthless for mankind.

Could there be more about Jesus than you ever realized? Paul writes in 1 Corinthians that God was reconciling the world through Jesus' life. For example, when Jesus was baptized, he didn't do it for himself, but for you and me. When Jesus walked in obedience to His Father, again HE didn't do it just for himself, but for you and me. When Jesus exercised faith, again HE also did it for you and me. The Incarnation is Jesus wrapping human flesh around his Godhead. From then onward, humanity became permanently connected with Jesus Christ. He entered humanity's darkness and walked out victorious for your sake and mine. As water baptism pictures, you and I are included with Christ in his life, death, and resurrection.

His ministry also restored the truth about His Father. Especially the mutual submissive love relationship which existed between both. Also, His personhood is the bridge that connects you and I with His Father. And since we are connected with Jesus, everything He has done or will do includes you and me. The Bible states approximately three hundred times that you and I are "in Christ." Such statements remind us that we have a personal union with Him. We take part with Him in His life. We are also incorporated with Him in fellowship with others. And most important, our identity is found in HIM. This is the Good News.

#110 – A Vicarious Life

"...that God was in Christ reconciling the world to Himself, not counting their trespasses against them..." 2 Corinthians 5:19 (NASB)

The entire life of Jesus Christ is more than any one event or situation. For many believers, we seem to focus on his miracles, teachings, death, and resurrection. All these are important. They reveal what Jesus' believed as He fulfilled Scripture as the Messiah. Yet when we focus only on portions of a person's life, we may often leave out the larger impact they leave behind.

As Paul writes in 2 Corinthians, God was reconciling the world to Himself through Jesus' life. Theologians call this the vicarious life - living life as a substitute for another. In Jesus' case, God became man clothing himself with humanity's flesh and blood. He took on mankind's skin.

What does this mean? It means everything HE did , HE did for us. As He worked, played, prayed, taught, and served others, HE did so as our substitute and for our sake. For example, His obedience toward our heavenly Father's Will He did as our substitute. The faith HE exercised HE did as our substitute. The love HE shared with others; HE did as our substitute. Even his death HE did as our substitute. Everything HE did, HE did as humanity's substitute before the eyes of our Heavenly Father.

So now when our heavenly Father looks at you and me, HE does so through the prism of Jesus' life. It is not solely our obedience or faith HE sees, but the obedience and faith of Jesus Christ. When we pray, Jesus takes those prayers as our High Priest before His Father. Our Father then hears them through the words of Jesus himself. Again, it is not our righteousness that the Father witnesses. But the righteousness of Jesus Christ that He sees.

Jesus Christ lived the vicarious life for you and me. Everything HE did, HE did so you and I can take part through Him with the Triune God in their eternal plan for mankind. C.S. Lewis called it the great dance. Two beings, one leading and the other following to the rhythm of the music around life's dance floor. Life the way God originally created it to be. And we don't have to be expert dancers to enjoy the journey. For He made it all possible. This is why we are thankful for the vicarious life Jesus lived for you and me.

#111 - What is Salvation All About?

"For the grace of God has appeared, bringing salvation for all people..." Titus 2:11

Salvation is not a prize, an event, nor a commodity. Salvation is the relationship you have in Jesus Christ with His Father via the Holy Spirit. You are included with Him in his life, death, resurrection, and ascension into heaven. This brings greater meaning to Who He IS and your participation with Him. That you are a new creation in Him. That you have been reconciled (saved) with His Father. That you are now connected with Jesus and the Father via the Holy Spirit - adopted into the Triune God circle. Yet to experience this new life, you need to change your thinking (repent.) You need to yield yourself to His authority (become his disciple). In so doing, you begin to experience the life (sanctification) that Jesus finished for you. The end result is eternal life (glorification) with Him in the new age.

You begin to experience this new life when you realize your identify is bound in Christ. Unlike the world's response, your identity is not found in yourself. But you are included in the personhood of Jesus Christ.

Apart from Christ, we usually start with our surroundings. We realize something must change in our lives, so we begin to change our environment. When that doesn't make a difference, we then work to modify our behavior. When that fails, we move toward increasing our capacity of knowledge or skill. After then, we may begin to clarify our beliefs. Lastly, we come to realize our identity of who we are is incorrect and needs adjusting.

But with Christ, we first begin with correctly identifying who we are in Him. We start at the top rather than move from the bottom to the top. From our relationship with Christ, our identity is now clarified. Our beliefs are aligned with reality. Our desire to grow in knowledge and skill is intensified; not for our sake but for the sake of others. Our attitude changes which leads to our behavior becoming more Christ-like. Then finally our environment becomes the breeding ground for ministry. We begin to express God's love and Kingdom ways for others to behold. We become a living testimony of God's workmanship. He is glorified. We reap the benefits. Others are introduced to the God of Jesus Christ.

Salvation is freedom with Christ. Free from loneliness, because you belong to Him. Free from fear, because His love penetrates through you. Free from anxiety, because His faith assures you. Free from sin's anguish, because His grace abounds in you.

Again, salvation is not a prize, event, nor commodity. Salvation is your relationship with Jesus Christ and His Father via the Holy Spirit. Salvation is Christ's finished work.

#112 – Hypocrisy

"Why do you see the speck that is in your brother's eye, but do not notice the log that is in your own eye?" Matt 7:3

Who among us is without sin? Who has never made a mistake in judgment? Who has not made a poor choice from a critical situation? Who among us hasn't lived up to God's expectations for us? When you find that person, let me know. For the fact is, everyone we meet is like you and me, imperfect. They may think they are perfect. They may act like they are perfect. But deep, down inside, they are hiding behind a log in their own eye. Hypocrites.

I can imagine when Jesus spoke these words, HE probably brought out a chuckle from the audience. People who live imperfect lives, know people who live in the illusion of perfection. These super righteous people establish high standards for themselves. The problem is they expect others to live by them. They forgive themselves when they can't live up to them. But they expound judgment toward those who fall short to their higher-than-God expectations. Hypocrites.

In fact, Jesus more than once gave a tongue lashing to the religious leaders of his day for being hypocrites. He even told his disciples to do what the religious leaders say to do, but don't follow their examples. Don't act like they do. For they don't do what they teach others to do. Hypocrites.

Hypocrites are blind to their own humanity. Instead of exercising mercy and grace like God does for us, they play the god of religion. They establish standards and regulations they find difficult to perform. But expect others to live by them. Hypocrites.

When Jesus is allowed to express Himself in you, you become disdained for the hypocrisy in you and others. Yet you are also thankful for the mercy and love God has bestowed upon you. So you gracefully share the same experience with others. You become more transparent in your relationship with others. You gain confidence in your walk with the Spirit and rejoice in the new creation that God is morphing in you.

You recognize the lie of hypocrisy in yourself and in others. So you first focus on removing the large beam you are carrying in your eye. Only then you help address the small splinter in your associate's eye. Isn't this what we do as we allow Jesus Christ to remove the hypocrisy in us as HE morphs you and me into his new creation?

#113 - What Is Worship?

"We know that God does not listen to sinners, but if anyone is a worshiper of God and does his will, God listens to him." John 9:31

Worship is the outer expression of your inner values. Jesus taught "For where your treasure is, there your heart will be also (MT. 6:21)." Thus, worship is expressing what you value most. The question is then: Who or what do you worship?

Every person worships someone or something. If you listen to yourself talk, you will discover what you worship. If your conversations are always filtered on a specific topic, you may have a hint. What is your favorite topic? Family. Money. Movies. People. Sex. Sports. Self. Business. Missions. Climate. Environment. Justice. Whatever topic is most important in your life may be what you worship.

As disciples of Jesus Christ, our primary focus is Him. As we invest more and more time with Him, we find ourselves speaking about Him or HIS Domain or HIS Spirit. We become more and more attuned to HIS ways and can't shut up if we tried. We want everyone to know Him and make Him known to others.

We praise Him in church services. We praise Him through our work. We praise Him in our relationship with others. Christ-centered worship is recognizing God in the situation you are in. It is giving Him the glory He deserves in what you are doing. When He is the center of every aspect of our life, then our life becomes a living sacrifice of worship to Him (Romans 12:1).

We worship Him as we pursue His Truth. We worship Him as we share our testimony with others. We worship Him as we surrender our lives to Him in service for others. As He matures us, we worship Him as His witness before others. Whatever we do in His Will, wherever we do it, and whenever we do it, we do so for His glory. This is our outer expression of the treasury in our inner heart toward Him. This is worship.

#114 - Problems, Trials, Obstacles

"...strengthening the souls of the disciples, encouraging them to continue in the faith, and saying that through many tribulations we must enter the kingdom of God." Acts 14.22

Question: what is one of the biggest illusions faith communities portray to the world? Answer: the Christian Life is free from pain, troubles, and heartaches.

I remember in my mid-thirties having a heated discussion with Mom. It was about being unprepared to handle the constant problems life throws at me. I grew up under the false assumption that life is a formula. When applied it will result in favorable outcomes. I soon realized my error. The only person prospering from such thinking were the authors. They and their publishers generated the propaganda to prosper their bank account.

Reality is such that life involves constant battles of survival. There are obstacles that need to be overcome. Most if not all are without guaranteed outcomes. Yet if someone had told me back then what I now know, would things turn out differently?

Maybe. Or maybe not. But it would have been more focused and life-generating.

The above Scripture was the outcome after the apostle Paul was left stoned to death a few days earlier. Presumed dead, his associates gathered him and brought him back to the city. There he arose the next day to preach the gospel to his audience. Did Paul know something we don't?

His message? "Through many tribulations we must enter the kingdom of God."

God doesn't necessary always prevent crap from happening in our life. But HE promises to walk through it with you. As HE joins us in the cesspool of life, we come to know him better, learn to communicate with him, and develop a trust in him. As we struggle to overcome, we are growing in character. We may also even redeem the situation for Him. You may also come into contact with others who will witness your patience and trust in Christ. You become a living testimony. When your Savior and Lord works out the mess you are in, you will discover more of his grace. After you walk through several of these undesirable situations, your faith is strengthen. You begin to realize how much God loves you.

Yes your circumstances may stink, but life is good. God not only resides in you, but is actively involved in morphing you into his divine image. You learn tribulations are the escalators God uses to strengthen and encourage us. He may also be doing the same with others as we walk with Him. Like an Olympic athlete, we appreciate the coach. We accept knowing we are being pushed and trained for bigger purposes. The trial turns into an event. A taste of God's Kingdom now while we wait for the full completion in the world tomorrow.

The circumstances and problems this life brings are designed to build trust in HIM. The process may be unnatural, but the outcome is definitely supernatural. So the next time you face problems, trials, and obstacles, remember the acronym A.S.A.P. Always. Stop. Ask. Pray.

Yes, we are learning from the Master Builder and Coach - Our Father-Son-Spirit. In the end, you may be surprised to find yourself peacefully rejoicing through the ordeal!

#115 - Today I Get To...

"Behold, what I have seen to be good and fitting is to eat and drink and find enjoyment in all the toil with which one toils under the sun the few days of his life that God has given him, for this is his lot." Ecclesiastes 5:18

Yes, I get too...
Experience God's love...
Play in our Heavenly Dad's worldwide sandbox...
Celebrate another day of discovery...
Communicate with the Creator of Life...
Enjoy the beauty of creation...
Serve others through work...
Work for his glory...
Earn income by serving others...
Pay bills...
Drink a cool glass of water...
Eat candy, cake, and cookies...
Smell chocolate covered raspberries...
Hug my bride...
Zoom with my daughter...
Ride a bicycle for pleasure and health...
Drive a car to the supermarket...
Plant a shrub...
Wash the windows...
Re-set the remote controller...

Watch football...

Read a book...

Trade the futures market...

Study passages from the Bible...

Attend a small Bible Study group...

Pray for our family, friends, and country...

Rejoice with a friend's accomplishments...

Grieve over the loss of a friend...

Exercise compassion for another...

Extend God's love with everyone we meet...

What about you? What are you fortunate, blessed, and grateful to do today?

#116 – This Christmas: Change The World With Christ

"He who was seated on the throne said, 'I am making everything new!'" Revelations 21:5

Everything begins and ends with Jesus Christ. He is the Alpha and the Omega. The First and the Last. He was there at the Big Bang. He was there when the earth was remodeled for the current age. And he will be there when we enter into the new age.

Christmas is a time to reflect on the beginning of HIS earthly arrival as the Lord of Lords and King of Kings. He entered the world as a babe some 2,000 years ago. But today HE resides as the first Man-Spirit in heaven. HE is humanity's Mediator between our Father God and us.

The Good News is God became Man. HE lived a vicarious life. HE died, was resurrected, and morphed into a spiritual being. His obedient life and death allows humanity to participate in his achievement. Today, being his follower means HE shares his wealth and accomplishments with us. His victory means victory for us. His life, death, and resurrection means life and resurrection for us. He calls us his brothers and sisters. We have been adopted into His Family.

As Christ-followers, we are now commissioned to make other disciples. All races and ethnic groups are included. Yes, everyone is included. As we accept who Jesus is, we serve Him as our King. As King, the entire world is HIS domain. Every social institution is answerable to Him. They may rebel against His authority, but then they will have to answer to His final judgment. For we have a King who has proven himself over and over again among his own.

He surrendered all to His heavenly Father when he left eternity to become a babe. He grew in stature before God and Man. He revealed his heavenly Father to us. Yes, Christmas isn't about family, presents, and self-indulgence anymore. Today it is about King Jesus preparing a people to rule and serve with Him.

God opened the doors for Him to share in His Father's Work. Today Jesus is allowing us to take part with Him in His Work. He is the reason for the season. He is still making everything new. But this time He is including you and me.

#117 - God's Purpose

"he made known to us the mystery of his will according to his good pleasure, which he purposed in Christ, to be put into effect when the times reach their fulfillment—to bring unity to all things in heaven and on earth under Christ." Eph 1:9-10 NIV.

In your walk with the Eternal, you will come to the realization your life purpose is not centered around you. The center is the Triune God. When one acknowledges this reality, the faster one discovers who they are in Christ. So for those who may have forgotten consider this a refresher course.

God's purpose is revealed throughout Scripture. Here are a few:

The restoration of creation back to His original intent. This follows the culmination of all things including the merging of a new heaven and new earth (Rev.22:1-5).

The adoption of humanity integrated into the home-life of the Triune God (Rm. 8:15, 23; 9:4; Eph. 1:5).

The expansion of His Kingdom government under the authority of Jesus Christ (Heb. 1:8; Lk.4:43).

The transformation of you and I into His (Jesus Christ) image for the sake of others and His glory (2 Corinth. 3:18; Phil.3:21).

In our walk with Father-Son-Spirit, we first focus on our personal salvation. Over time, we come to realize our salvation is the opportunity to take part with God's Family Business. That sin was only a hiccup in God's plan to birth an Eternal family. That when we focus on a relationship with our Heavenly Father, we discover more who we are. That we also find out how we are wired to serve in the Family Business.

God's Plan isn't centered around you nor I. We were created to take part with Him in His plan. So if you haven't done so yet, ask Him to show you where and how you can best serve the King of Kings. You will be surprised where you end up!

#118 - Why Theology Matters?

"Now these Jews were more noble than those in Thessalonica; they received the word with all eagerness, examining the Scriptures daily to see if these things were so." Acts 17:11

Theology is about the study of God. Like other fields of study, there are proven methods and techniques to help one learn. When followed, one accumulates knowledge, understanding, and wisdom of the subject matter.

So why is the study of theology important?

Because good theology draws you closer to the God who created reality. Good theology opens one's eyes to know more about Him. Good theology is the basis of building a strong framework for life. When applied, one's life becomes more physically, socially, and spiritually richer.

Poor theology distorts your relationship with the Creator. So your potential to live a full, meaningful life is reduced. Instead of living your potential, poor theology robs you from fully knowing yourself. Poor theology focuses more on illusion rather than reality.

The further one is away from the core of reality, the further one's theology of God becomes distorted.

Good theology comes from living the with-God life. Bad theology (or no theology) is living life by keeping God a distance away from you. Good theology hugs God every time you meet. Poor theology is pushing God away.

When one begins to develop a relationship with the Author of Life, they want to know everything about Him. And the more you hang out with Him, the more He reveals Himself to you.

Don't be afraid of theology. Everyone is a theologian. The question is which type do you want to be?

#119 - Escape or Engagement

"Your kingdom come. Your will be done, on earth as it is in heaven." Matthew 6:10

There are those in the faith whose purpose for living is to do as little now as possible. They seek to escape from this life into heaven. But there are those who understand their mission is to now colonize earth. To place their corner of the world under the kingdom of God domain. I coin these as either escape or engagement theology.

Under the escape mentality, it's all about getting off this planet and into heaven. Of course, as quickly as possible under Biblical scrutiny. The engagement mindset though is to live out kingdom rule now. They engage with the cultural around them until God's kingdom is fully restored on earth.

I always wondered about Jesus' prayer model. Why HE emphasized God's kingdom and Will to take charge on earth and not pray for us to escape earth. Later on, HE did request we escape from the temptations of evil, but again not from planet earth. Instead HIS desire was for his disciples to focus on earth as their mission. They are to share His teachings with others and be a witness for others of God's work in their lives. His desire was for his apprentices to engage the culture around them.

So if your desire has been to escape rather than deal with the culture, ask God to change your heart and eyes. To find ways for his kingdom to expand in your corner of the world. You will discover a side of the Holy Spirit that will recharge your focus. You will also increase your motivation to serve our great King.

Let's seek engagement, not escapism as we testify what God is doing in our life today.

#120 - Business Is Ministry

"There are different kinds of service, but the same Lord." 1 Corinthians 12:5 NIV.

Sometimes we cause problems for others without realizing the impact of our words. Those who have a platform to influence others will give an account for their work. This includes Church pastors, Bible teachers, and ignorant believers.

I include ignorant believers with pastors and teachers. Why? Because at times they may be ignorant of the subject matter. This is so true when it comes to the Body of Christ outside of the four walls of an organized faith community.

Who stated that Pastors and missionaries are the most important roles in the world today? That CEO's, government leaders, and moms are secondary in God's eyes. What does the Bible reveal? So let's step back and valuate the importance of each.

Jesus himself stated that man does not live by bread alone but with every word that comes from the mouth of God. He didn't elevate one over the other. HE considered both important for the human experience.

The church mission is important. So is the mission of business. The mission of education. The mission of government. And all other institutions that serve people. If people didn't provide for the physical substance we need, would we even consider God's word?

Business is a ministry because business serves the needs of people. The word ministry means service. God instructed us to serve one another. We serve one another by providing material and spiritual food for each other. We serve one another by sharing and adding value to God's creation.

All the gifts of the Holy Spirit also operate outside the four walls of a church community. The gift of leadership is exercised as a witness within the public forum. Like any gift, it may be used to glorify God or for selfish pursuit. Whether behind a pulpit or a corporate boardroom, the gifts of the Holy Spirit are there to be shared. They are the means of serving others and glorifying God. They can be used destructively for personal gain or beneficially for serving others.

Church is in session outside of the four walls of a faith community for more hours than one hour Sunday morning. The only difference pertains to how sermons are being preached. These business leaders speak with their attitudes and actions. They are letting their faith shine in the workplace with good work. Instead of praising God through music, they are praising God through their service. They are creating new start-ups, jobs, and products for the masses.

Contrary to many pastors there are many different ways to conduct a church service. They may have gone through their denominational, institutional training and learned one way. What they may be comfortable with is only one way.

Is it possible a business model led by Spirit-filled believers could also be a church service? A place to worship our great God? A place to learn how faith, love, and hope play out in the real world? A place where the offering is self-sacrificing service to others?

Sometimes we need to take a step back and look at how BIG our God is and realize that the world is our pastoral home. That business is only another way for believers to serve their King, His subjects, and His domain. God's world, His church, and His people can change the culture around them. But only when the Body of Christ removes their self-imposed limits. Imagine what could happen if we allow God's Kingdom to expand outside the four walls of a faith community.

About the Author

After stewarding senior leadership roles with several national organizations, Mike now serves as an adjunct professor with a local faith-based university, active with Stephen Ministry, and facilitates small groups within his faith community. He holds a PhD in pastoral ministry and a graduate degree in management.

His passion is to engage, encourage, and empower others to become firmly rooted in Jesus Christ for the advancement of God's Kingdom through the local Church and marketplace.

In his personal time, Mike enjoys biking, day trading, and huddling with family and friends.

Read more at https://radicalinchrist.com.

Milton Keynes UK
Ingram Content Group UK Ltd.
UKHW020923231123
433129UK00016B/1040